CONTENTS

AUTHOR'S NOTE

While I was well aware of the lengthy and involved nature of the
Whitesnake story, some of the complex behind the scenes goings-on
surprised even me. It's been fascinating delving into it, and I hope if
you're a Whitesnake fan it'll be equally interesting to read. I was keen to
avoid the usual over-reliance on old press articles when putting the story
together, so I'd like to thank the people who made this possible.

Among the musicians, foremost credit has to go to Neil Murray.
Ever since the guy tried to buy my silver jacket off me after a
Whitesnake show many moons ago, it was clear that here was a musician
who had managed to survive in the business while keeping both feet
planted firmly on the ground (give or take the odd tumble in the dry-ice).
Neil also belongs to that select group of bassists (why is it always the
bassist?) who document their musical careers, keeping diaries, pictures
etc. This was also a great help. Another bassist who deserves thanks is
Malcolm Buckton who spoke at length about Coverdale's early days
before fame and fortune took him away from the salt and sea air of Tees-
side. Like Neil, Malcolm also hoarded ephemera about those days and
this I'm sure will fascinate Coverdale fans old and new.

I'd also like to thank Micky Moody for his time, Cozy Powell
for his help, Roger Barker, the Rockline Radio Network and that dynamic
duo of ex-managers, Tony Edwards and John Coletta. Away from the
profession as it were, Ann Warburton let me off the chores while I burnt
the midnight oil. Di Mather and Mark Maddock both read and corrected
early drafts. Peter Weisner from Germany, Steve Wunrow, John Barnes,
Mike Havener and Shari York in America, Mike Eriksson in Sweden all
helped in one way or another, as did France's finest, Dominique and
Thierry Pierron. Lorraine Pickering dug about to unearth The Fabulosa
Brothers and Rosie Hardman filled me in on Mel Galley. Pete Frame's
Rock Family Trees and Terry Hounsome's *Rock Record* have never been far
from my reach during the proceedings.

My thanks to the unknown service person who put my Amstrad PCW
back together when it began to give under the strain, to Backyard Films
for the xerox facilities and to Chris Charlesworth for all his help.

There appears at present to be no fan-club for the band, official
or otherwise, since the demise of Snakebite. However, plans for one in
Germany exist and I'd be happy to put interested people in touch. In the
meantime the UK Deep Purple Appreciation Society (from which much
of the memorabilia in this book was loaned) continues to provide
coverage of all the members of the group including David Coverdale.
Reach them (or me) at: PO Box 254, Sheffield S6 1DF,
South Yorkshire, UK.

CHAPTER I

1951-1976

THE EARLY DAYS

Saltburn is a small seaside town on the North East coast of England. Below it sit pretty fishing villages, which have become increasingly reliant on the tourist industry for their livelihoods, while above, industrial coastal development begins in earnest at Middlesborough and continues to expand as you travel northwards. Saltburn sits uneasily between the two. Over the years attempts have been made to develop it as a holiday resort; the magnificent station building is evidence of how visitors were expected to arrive and the sea front has Victorian guest houses as grand and uncompromising as any on the south coast.

Doubtless it enjoyed a brief heyday as a result of all this effort but today's car driving trippers pass by on the way to more attractive resorts further down the coast. Maternity homes belong to a more leisured age as well and Overdean in Saltburn disappeared in the late seventies, swallowed up by the Cleveland Area Health Authority, the building sold and the grounds divided up for redevelopment. It was here on September 22, 1951 that David Coverdale was born. His first home was a small club in the town run by his parents.

An only child, he was educated at the Huncliffe County Modern School on the edge of town and made his first stage appearance at school when he was just five, performing a medley of Tommy Steele tunes standing on top of his desk. Back home, via the juke-box in the club, Coverdale was turned on at an early age by some of the most influential of the British bands of the mid to late sixties – The Pretty Things, The Sorrows, The Yardbirds and The Kinks, whose 'You Really Got Me' classic remains a favourite to this day. One wonders if the fact that Jon Lord tinkled the ivories on the record had any bearing on future events. There was also Jimi Hendrix, his passion for whom went as far as getting him into fights with less musically educated boys.

Coverdale's interests in art and Greek mythology ("I could answer all the mythology questions on University Challenge when I was 14") had to be worked on but singing seemed to come naturally. He remembers his first 'electric' appearance when he played at the Red Lodge Social Club on Boxing Day 1967 and got paid for it. From school with a couple of 'O' Levels under his belt, Coverdale went to the Green Lane Art College in Middlesborough, travelling up each day from Marske where his family moved after closing down their club. He fancied being an artist but soon switched to a Graphic Design course, with a bit of teacher training thrown in. There he began to rub shoulders with other musically inclined people, first with Vintage 67, about whom memories appear to have faded altogether, then to more purpose in a blues band called Denver Mule, formed by a few friends he'd made in school and college. The year was 1967 and he was 16-years-old.

Coverdale took any opportunity to further his musical education, including the occasional gig with Magdalene (who later got Chris Rea in on vocals and became The Beautiful Losers, achieving fame locally after winning a *Melody Maker* pop contest), but he found the prospect of several years at college harder to handle, especially financially. He certainly wasn't going to make his fortune with Denver Mule however, and towards the end of 1968 they decided to call it a day, playing their last show at Kirby College. Word of Coverdale's singing abilities had got around though and in the crowd to catch that last show was Malcolm Buckton, bassist with The Skyliners.

The Skyliners assembled in 1963 just as the beat group boom was taking off and groups were replacing the traditional dance bands which had held sway for so many years. This group was the brain child of Roger Barker and a pal from Cleveland Tech, but Barker found his spare time increasingly swallowed up by his involvement with the Redcar Jazz Club so he left to concentrate on that. The band's vocalist, Norrie Roy, also gave it up and so for a time their guitarist found he had to handle the vocal chores as well. With the addition of sax and trumpet, the need for a proper singer arose, hence Buckton's appearance at that Denver Mule concert. "I was very impressed, so we got him down the next week and gave him an audition."

Coverdale was keen for the gig, especially as The Skyliners were making pretty good money for a semi-professional group, but opinions were divided as to whether he was right for the kind of shows the band were doing at the time. "There was no question of his capabilities as a singer at all," Malcolm Buckton recalled. "In the end we said let's give him a try and see how it goes." So after turning him down initially Coverdale was offered the job on a trial basis in November 1968.

As his interest in college began to wane Coverdale spent more and more time hanging around the Purple Onion coffee bar in Middlesborough and it was here that he first met up with guitarist Micky Moody, then with Tramline. Moody recalled his first sight of David many years later . . . "He used to go about wearing a donkey jacket and a very risqué complexion." Tramline was signed to Island Records which immediately put them a couple of rungs further up the ladder than most local groups. Once Coverdale had got to know Moody, he was taken on as an unofficial roadie on two occasions when the band travelled down to play the Marquee Club in London where Island had them supporting fairly regularly.

Coverdale's audition period with The Skyliners won over any doubts they may have had and he joined permanently. Having done so, Coverdale decided to jack college in and trust to his musical career to see him through. The one thing everyone recalls clearly about Coverdale during these early days was that his determination and belief that he would make it marked him out from most other local musicians. Right now though, he was soon in debt. "Roger Barker lent him a brand new AKG mike and he got so involved in his singing he broke it the first night." With funds short the band arranged a loan to purchase his own mike, stopping £2 out of his wages each week to pay for it. "I could buy a bloody album for that," was Coverdale's response.

The Skyliners were certainly a busy band, with Roger Barker getting them supporting slots at the Redcar Jazz Club whenever he could (on only his second gig with the group Coverdale found himself supporting Joe Cocker there) as well as the numerous halls in the area. Before long the name Skyliners was deemed to be somewhat dated and after some attempts to pick a new one, during which they almost became Django at Coverdale's suggestion, a friend hit on the name The Government, inspired by the new health warnings on cigarette packets. While the band's work load was sufficient for most of the members – nearly all of whom had day jobs – Coverdale was surviving on his income from the group and was always short of money

David Coverdale *(far right)* with The Government in their 'informal' stage attire . . .

despite living at home. Their bassist managed to get him a job at a local timber yard making window frames. "I don't think he got a full week in, his excuse for leaving was that the other lads were putting chewing gum in his hair," he said.

Musically Coverdale found it hard to adjust totally to The Government's work load at first. Some nights they would be doing cabaret spots at prestigious night clubs as far afield as Manchester, on other occasions they would be playing entirely different material for college or university audiences.

Not surprisingly it was the cabaret stuff which caused him the most trouble. Malcolm Buckton remembered, "We used to have to dress him up and get him to sing the stuff and yet he was such a good singer, he used to do 'Phoenix' and 'Yesterday'. The classic was 'Joanna', the Scott Walker song, he sang that beautifully." It was at the less formal shows that Coverdale really enjoyed himself. Again they used to do mainly covers but this time it was material like Black Sabbath's 'Paranoid', stuff by T.Rex and even a few Deep Purple tracks like 'Hush' and later 'Black Night'.

Indeed on one occasion in 1969 The Government

. . . and *(top centre)* in formal attire. "We had to dress him ourselves!" bassist Malcolm **Buckton** *(far right)* recalls.

The original Deep Purple line-up, 1968. *(L–R)* Blackmore, Lord, Evans, Simper and Paice.

found themselves supporting Deep Purple down at Bradford University although they didn't find out about it until they arrived. Jon Lord and Roger Glover were impressed enough to sit through their sound check, applauding a beefy version of 'Shaking All Over', but Coverdale's lingering memory of the evening was when Ian Gillan came up to him after they'd done their set. "You sang well," he told him, "but your PA ruined you."

The following year The Government auditioned for the BBC in Manchester to play on *Radio One Club*, a regular show which consisted of discs, guests and a live band all recorded before an audience. It was useful experience but Coverdale had taken to spending his free evenings staying up late listening to albums, then sleeping in the following day, so the band made sure a roadie stayed the night just to be certain he was up in time to get down to wherever the show was being taped.

Coverdale, a few years younger than the others, used to tell people he was an apprentice pop singer when anyone asked. In some ways he was still a little green and open to having the micky taken when the others had a mind. One evening they took particular delight at Coverdale's consternation when the transit began the long haul up the steep hill leading from a gig in the coastal resort of Whitby. Sensing his apprehension, the band opened the van doors, "just in case they had to get out quick if the brakes failed." The driver lurched down through the gear box and eventually Coverdale, unable to take it any longer, leapt over his passengers and out of the door, whereupon they put the pedal to the floor and took off leaving him cursing.

The band's reputation brought opportunities to back people like Elkie Brooks and The Paper Dolls (hard to imagine Coverdale singing 'Gimme Dat Ding'

with a girl trio) and began to attract agents with offers of full-time work both here and abroad. Eventually the band felt that it was all getting a little too much and early in 1971 agreed to come off the road for a break and make a decision about whether or not to turn professional.

In view of this they decided to use some of the group funds to record a single as a memento for themselves and friends. They finished work after a show at an RAF base in Lincoln on February 20 and two days later trooped into the Multicord Studios in Sunderland to lay down four tracks. As they were paying out of their own pockets, the idea was to get it done as quickly as possible but they'd reckoned without Coverdale who kept pushing for just one more take of his vocals. "There was an argument in the end and he said something about, 'If this is something I'm going to keep for the rest of me life I want it right'," Malcolm Buckton recalls. Twenty-five copies were pressed up and The Government took that well deserved rest.

The members decided not to turn professional and instead to restrict their playing mainly to weekends as more of a recreational pursuit than anything else. Today they can still be found gigging locally at clubs in the area. This decision posed a problem for Coverdale, who had now left home and was living in Alma Parade in Redcar. His pop lifestyle hadn't squared well with his father who was doing shift work at a local steel mill. When another local band called Harvest offered him a gig on a trip they were planning to Denmark he took it, even though the band were far from perfect. A couple of weeks sleeping rough in the van was more than enough and, spending what he'd earned on a ferry ticket home, he returned to Redcar.

Musically things were now rather bleak and when a friend gave him a chance to learn the clothes trade at a boutique in Middlesborough called 36 he took it. Not long after, he began work at an offshoot of the Gentry boutique in Redcar called Stride, where he proved a more than able salesman, shifting Falmers flares and cheesecloth tops. He joined a Santana influenced local group called Rivers Invitation and he and a couple of the other members also used to perform as part of the house band at the Starlite Club in Redcar, which in those days was mainly the talents of bassist Colin

The classic line-up, Blackmore, Gillan, Glover, Paice and Lord, during the Fireball album sessions, 1971.

Hodgkinson and sax man Ronnie Asprey.

Early in 1973 Coverdale was asked to do a charity show at the local Leonard Cheshire home. Initially he planned to do it himself, playing guitar and singing, but decided to recruit another guitarist, then a drummer and a bass player, some of whom had been in Rivers Invitation. Billed as The Fabulosa Brothers, they had such a good time that they decided to gig once a week in a pub called The Wheatsheaf and later landed another residency at The Coatham Hotel.

Their guitarist, Alan Fearnley (whose band The Real McCoy had often crossed paths with The Government), owned a record shop in Middlesborough and they used to rehearse there, while their other guitarist Austin McLoughlin also worked in a record store locally. Between the pair of them they had many contacts with the music business and a few demo tapes were produced with a view to a possible record deal but nothing came of it. Coverdale was busy writing in his spare time too; songs like 'Holy Man', 'Sail Away' and 'Soldier Of Fortune', all of which he would later lay down with Deep Purple, began life during this time.

Stories of Deep Purple's impending split and the departure of vocalist Ian Gillan surfaced in the press in June of that year and it was a sarcastic remark from someone in the boutique that inspired Coverdale to have a bash at securing an audition – he had after all very little to lose and hoped they might recall their meeting four years before. His point of contact was again Roger Barker, who through his role booking acts into the Jazz Club, was able to get through to Purple's offices.

While the secretary was somewhat shirty, more interested initially in how the number had been obtained, Roger Barker was told to get a tape in the post, so the infamous Fabulosa Brothers tape joined the ever growing pile of demos down at Purple's offices in London. Three weeks later, impressed by the way Coverdale had tackled the material on the demo (which he later admitted was probably due as much to what he'd been drinking before the tapes rolled as anything else), he was invited down to London for a proper audition. They remembered The Government but couldn't recall what the singer looked like, so a photo was hastily put in the post. Roger Barker actually accompanied Coverdale on the trip down to Scorpio Studios near Euston Station for the simple reason that, ''He couldn't find his way out of Middlesborough.''

The rest is history as they say. On December 8, 1973, Coverdale was fronting Deep Purple for the first

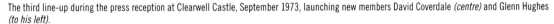

The third line-up during the press reception at Clearwell Castle, September 1973, launching new members David Coverdale *(centre)* and Glenn Hughes *(to his left)*.

time, in Sweden. At first he was somewhat overawed by his new-found circumstances – Jon Lord tells of the times he saw David in the wings listening to the soloing along with the rest of the audience as if he weren't really part of it all. "I was a little boy lost when I first joined the band but I became an egomaniac after six months," he later confessed. His days with the band are well documented in *Deep Purple: The Illustrated Biography* by Chris Charlesworth (Omnibus Press, 1983).

After recording the 'Burn' album, Deep Purple went on to become the biggest selling band in America the following year. With Glenn Hughes, David Coverdale was instrumental in keeping the band going after the departure of Ritchie Blackmore in 1975 but his admiration for Tommy Bolin was soon tempered by frustration at the guitarist's inability to grasp his new situation. At the end of 1975 the band set off on a world tour which went from bad to worse; by the time they reached Britain they were falling apart at the seams. The dream had become a nightmare. As he walked off stage at the Liverpool Empire in March, he walked out of the band for good. "I was frightened to leave the band. Purple was my life, Purple gave me my break but all the same I wanted out," he later admitted.

Jon Lord.

Top: Tommy Bolin.
Middle: Ian Paice.
Bottom: Glenn Hughes.

CHAPTER II

1976-April 1977

POST DEEP PURPLE
TO FIRST SOLO LP

Previous Page: David Coverdale recording Wizard's Convention album, 1976, following his departure from Deep Purple.

Following Coverdale's decision to quit Deep Purple, things went very quiet. The band's management accepted his resignation but hoped to salvage something from the situation and told Coverdale to keep it strictly to himself for the time being. This wasn't too difficult as Purple were due for a long break following the world tour in any case. Guitarist Tommy Bolin returned to the States almost at once. He had his solo career waiting, with a follow-up to his excellent 'Teaser' album to prepare. Indeed he hoped to use some members of Deep Purple on it but problems over work permits would prevent this.

Drummer Ian Paice, who had at times almost single handedly carried the band when things were at their very worst on-stage, took off to make plans for his forthcoming marriage. The others gathered in London as guests of Eddie Hardin who was recording a new album, produced by Roger Glover, which eventually surfaced as 'The Wizards Convention' later that year (though you could be forgiven for missing it, so low-key was the release).

Eddie Hardin, as one half of the Hardin/York duo, had supported Deep Purple in the early seventies and kept in touch with Glover ever since. Free of the worries of the past few months, the Deep Purple members were now able to relax and play simply as session musicians; Jon Lord helped out on piano, Glenn Hughes sang on a couple of tracks and David Coverdale ended up contributing an excellent vocal for a song called on 'Money To Burn'. It seemed to come from the heart. Given the extraordinary financial problems his departure from Deep Purple was about to land him in, the emotion he gave to the recording is all the more understandable; it remains one of his finest studio performances to date.

The session over, Glenn Hughes also took off for America, to rejoin his old mates in the newly reformed Trapeze on an American tour, setting the pattern for over a decade of projects which, to the dismay of his fans, always seemed to fold just as they were about to bear fruit. Jon Lord, burdened by the breakdown of his seven-year marriage as well as the collapse of Deep Purple, went off to join Ian Paice and finalise plans for a new group, while David Coverdale began work on a solo album. Thus it was that by the time the managers had scripted a press release in mid-July announcing the final demise of Deep Purple, the band members themselves were already immersed in new projects.

For David Coverdale the two years following the end of Deep Purple were a frustrating and worrying time and it wasn't until 1978 that he would be able to perform on-stage again. He had no great wish to pursue a solo career as such, preferring to work in a band situation. The idea of doing a solo album arose during discussions with, and at the suggestion of, the Deep Purple management for, although Coverdale had resigned from Deep Purple the group, he was still tied to Deep Purple the company.

What Coverdale had failed to realise during the superstar lifestyle he had enjoyed over the last three years was that he was actually paying for it. The enormous cost of running Deep Purple was funded from monies accrued from the earnings of the individuals concerned. This was fine for the members of the previous line-up who were able to live well off income generated by previous albums and tours but it was to be some time before Coverdale would begin to see royalties from his contributions to the band. He was in effect living on credit. Had he continued for a few more years with Deep Purple the situation would probably have evened itself out but, resigning when he did, the cash flow situation was erratic to say the least.

Despite this, Coverdale began plans for a solo recording. Just prior to Deep Purple's last Wembley concerts, he phoned up an old mate, Micky Moody, then busy doing sessions following the demise of Snafu. It had been two years since they'd spoken, Moody having bid Coverdale farewell during a small gathering

Glenn Hughes recording vocals for Wizard's Convention, before leaving to set up home in America.

Recording the track Money To Burn, one of the highlights of the Wizard's Convention album.

he'd held prior to leaving for his first American tour with Deep Purple. "He called and said I'm doing a solo album, would you like to play on it?" Moody was chuffed at the idea, envisaging an all-star gathering of guitarists like Blackmore and Beck. "I said I'd love to play on a few tracks and he said, 'No, I want you to do all of it, write it with me'." Moody was taken aback, fearing a wind-up. Assured it wasn't, they agreed to meet at the Wembley shows.

The problems within Purple were well shielded from the outside world and Moody expected to see a proper superstar band at work. "But after the gig he just shot off, said 'Let's go', he couldn't wait to get away, he'd had enough. I was quite shocked." Once he saw the situation and realised the project was serious, Micky Moody went into it wholeheartedly.

Coverdale decamped to Germany once Deep Purple's tour ended, staying at the Arabella Hotel in Munich. The management agreed to fund a solo record, provided he didn't go wild in the studio so he began writing. Every so often Moody would go over and they'd spend time together working on the music.

Germany had been chosen by Coverdale mainly for personal reasons. He wanted to be near his girlfriend Julia (Jools) and her two children, John and Dembreigh and after a time they managed to rent a house at Herrsching on the banks of the Ammersee. It looked impressive in the photographs but they had to leave most of it unfurnished until the financial situation improved. The two had met back in 1974 in Germany after the performance of Jon Lord's eccentric 'Windows' concert, which featured both David Coverdale and Glenn Hughes.

The conductor of the orchestra for the evening, Eberhard Schoener, had invited her to a restaurant where in a home-made dress which her daughter described simply as "very exciting", David Coverdale was for once stuck for words. Julia Borkowski had been married to an American painter called Jack Cody but they had been divorced back in 1968. Although some years older than Coverdale, with her he found a stability which life since joining Deep Purple four years ago had denied him. As the album sleeve notes explained, once he was settled in these more relaxed surroundings, he felt able to write somewhat less morose material in a style which harked back to the music he enjoyed before joining Deep Purple.

While Coverdale was setting up home in Germany, Jon Lord and Ian Paice flew out to discuss their ideas for a new band and tried to persuade him to join. David decided against it, publicly because instead of being known by the acronym PAL it would have become CLAP, but more probably because he wasn't entirely sure teaming up with them was the right thing to do.

Coverdale remained in touch however and not long after returned to England for Ian Paice's wedding where he met members of Deep Purple for the first time since the UK concerts and discovered nobody had told Hughes or Bolin that he had quit. The music for that first David Coverdale solo album was actually taped in London over two weeks in early August 1976 using a scratch band of session players at Kingsway Recorders, owned by former Deep Purple vocalist Ian Gillan.

Gillan had invested in a number of projects after leaving the group: a luxury hotel, a British motorcycle engine, a firm of hire cars and the studio. By the time this album was done only the studio remained viable. Roger Glover was the resident producer. He began learning the ins and outs of the mixer desk almost as soon as he joined Deep Purple and even while they were working flat out, Glover often spent any free time doing production work. One of his first jobs had been the début album for Elf, Ronnie Dio's old band, after

Micky Moody, fellow Geordie enlisted by Coverdale to help record his first solo album.

which he had gone on to produce Nazareth, Rory Gallagher, Ian Gillan and many more.

For Coverdale's album Glover himself handled synthesiser and shared the bass work with De Lisle Harper. Simon Phillips, a session drummer in great demand at the time with credits ranging from the Lloyd Webber 'Evita' album to Phil Manzanera's '801', Tim Hinkley on keyboards and of course Micky Moody on guitar, formed the nucleus of the group. Moody's musical contribution to the album was in fact considerable, his credit appearing alongside David's on four of the nine tracks. The sleeve acknowledges his and Glover's help . . . 'Without Micky Moody an' Roger, I would have had to do it on me own. GOD BLESS 'EM.'

There were also assorted guests, notably Ron Asprey on sax, a man both Coverdale and Moody had admired in his days at the Redcar Jazz Club. Once the backing tracks were done, the tapes were flown over to Musicland Studios in Munich. Coverdale had spent much of his recording career with Deep Purple here; their 'Stormbringer' and 'Come Taste The Band' albums had been laid down at Musicland. He did the vocals for the album over four days at the end of August and the results were taken back to London for Roger Glover to mix down during the first week of September.

Micky Moody went back to preparing material for an album of his own and Coverdale waited to see what his next move should be. His management were not keen to see him back on the road and wanted to keep him available to promote the solo album when it came out. They also wanted to know where the hit single was. To counter this, Coverdale mailed them a cassette demo of a new song called 'Sweet Mistreater' which seemed to fit the bill. The problem was that most of the session people used on the album were now busy elsewhere, and by the time the track was done it was too late to get the album issued ahead of the traditional Christmas rush of vinyl rubbish.

Coverdale was anxious to work live again. Unable to finance a band, he checked out other openings. Rumours circulated round the business that he was poised to take over Ozzy Osbourne's slot in Black Sabbath (not the last time his name would be linked with theirs). Happily this was not the case but he did rehearse with Uriah Heep, though he felt afterwards that while it might have been worthwhile financially, artistically it wouldn't do a great deal for him. He also received another offer around this time, a job with an unnamed group comprising Willy Weeks, Andy Newmark, Jean Roussel and guitarist Jeff Beck.

Coverdale was in no doubt as to his decision on this one but, as is often the case with Beck, the project folded before he got to jam with them. Coverdale's only foray on to the stage during this period in limbo was a jam with Nazareth who were touring Germany. "It may not sound fantastic to have gone on-stage with them but it was the first time they'd ever allowed anyone to do so. Add to that the fact that I was so frustrated not being able to do gigs, it was great.''

The album was finally issued early in 1977 in both Germany and France. His manager pulled a few strings to secure Coverdale a slot on French TV to promote it, miming over one of the tracks. "We were due to arrive at the TV station at about 10 in the evening,

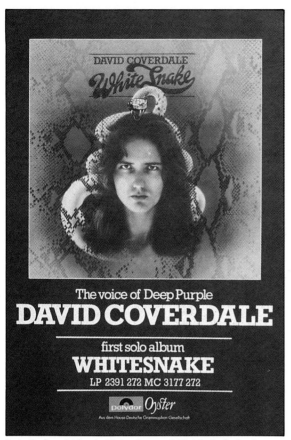

The voice of Deep Purple
DAVID COVERDALE
first solo album
WHITESNAKE
LP 2391 272 MC 3177 272

polydor Oyster
Aus dem Hause Deutsche Grammophon Gesellschaft

Poster for Coverdale's solo début – air gun pellet hole in the forehead c/o producer Roger Glover.

which we did. They messed us around for nearly two hours and eventually began taping the four-minute song at about three minutes to 12 and then, at 12 o'clock suddenly all the switches were thrown and French television went on strike.''

In Britain the album was delayed until a single could be recorded after which they decided to go for an album track instead. 'Hole In The Sky' and the album, still on the Purple label, dressed in a nicely designed sleeve and titled simply 'David Coverdale's Whitesnake' hit British stores in May 1977 to universal . . . well, indifference is probably the only word for it.

The music press was in turmoil, reflecting the upheavals in the industry generally. Up until now, they had by and large served all types of rock music fairly evenly but the arrival of punk changed all that. Many writers simply couldn't handle the new scene, others came in on the bandwagon but developed an insecurity as they did so, worried that they might be untrendy, quick to bury bands they'd been championing only weeks before. Suddenly all that had gone before was simply uncool.

There were a few reviewers willing to give it a whirl though and generally those that did were fair. ''We're provided with undeniable evidence of Coverdale's strength as a soloist,'' wrote *NME* but Coverdale seemed ''unsure what to do with his remarkable voice now he's got his second big break. Obscurity beckons dangerously,'' they added by way of warning. Not everyone was so down about it: Joe Cocker was keen to

do a version of 'Peace Loving Man' for example, while Rod Stewart expressed an interest in murdering, sorry, covering 'Hole In The Sky'.

Photo shoots set up in Germany featuring a real python threatened to turn nasty – probably when it spotted Coverdale's jacket was trimmed with real snakeskin. The keepers managed to calm the snake down, though Whitesnake's career might never have got off the ground had it had the courage of its convictions.

With hindsight, the overriding impression of the album is of a set of polished demos, tracks which given the work afforded later material, might have stood the test of time a little better. The album reflects the circumstances under which it was assembled. It certainly wasn't the go-for-it set most people expected. Often Coverdale sounds unrelaxed and not sure what to do with his voice, as if he's holding back, while mixing him down didn't help. Certainly towards the end of his Purple days his singing suffered and he seems not to have found himself again as he taped this. The backings sound like the session jobs they were, the drumming often suspect.

A year before Coverdale sang on one of the hardest and funkiest rock sets Deep Purple ever generated and the change could hardly have been more pronounced. Micky Moody's influence is clear and he helped write most of the up-tempo songs; the more reflective material was mainly David's alone. ''He told me, I want to do an album of stuff I really like, I want to do rock, soul, ballads, 'cos David can sing anything – and that's what the album was basically, bits of Little Feat and everything.''

Some of it still works. 'Blindman', a slow Free-like composition, builds nicely helped by Glover's keyboard, while the title track kicks up the pace too. 'Hole In The Sky', a simple but moving track, sees Coverdale nailing the emotion of the moment though it was an unlikely choice for a single. 'Sunny Days', written about Deep Purple's last American tour, boogies along nicely. Coverdale also explained that the chorus to 'Peace Loving Man' was about his feelings during Deep Purple's final days. In fact three of the numbers had originally been intended for the next Deep Purple album: 'Lady' and 'Time On My Side' were the others.

Promotion was limited. There were no concerts and plans for him to do *The Old Grey Whistle Test* were called off. He did the round of local radio stations instead, plugging the album and chatting about life beyond Deep Purple. Naturally many of the interviewers pressed him on that area and the inevitable 'Voice Of Deep Purple' tag which some countries had seen fit to plaster across the sleeve to try and boost sales. ''I'm not over-happy with it but I can't deny it. For the rest of my life, I'll have that affiliation.''

Coverdale seemed keen to get it off his chest, though to fan the flames he did add that there were already plans for Deep Purple to reform before the year was up, albeit for a one-off charity show. The single disappeared without trace and the album failed to achieve anything more than modest sales (figures are notoriously well guarded but an estimate of something like 2,000 copies was given at the time). They couldn't even secure a deal for America.

CHAPTER III

April 1977 - Early 1978

'NORTHWINDS' TO WHITESNAKE Mk 1

Even while Coverdale was out and about promoting the first LP, the finishing touches were being made to the follow-up which was started at Air Studios in London during March and April 1977. "It's frustrating having to wait for the second one," he explained during interviews. "It's very difficult to think back and talk sensibly about the first album." Again the vocals were recorded at Musicland during the middle of April, though this time the tapes were mixed there as well.

Once more it was Micky Moody who helped out with the writing and most of the musicians were recalled with the addition of Tony Newman on drums and Alan Spenner on bass. Roger Glover stuck mainly to production apart from some synthesiser work. For backing vocals he used the Chanter Sisters, although for one song he added a chorus featuring Ronnie Dio and his wife Wendy, Jon Lord's wife and both Roger Glover and his wife Judi, along with his own future wife Julia and her son – 'The class of 77'.

Listening to tapes of the second album in May of 1977 I could well understand the frustration he must have felt at having to keep it on ice for so long for it was so much better than the first. He also relished the prospect of working live once again. "I'm hoping I'll be able to form a touring band of the same musical calibre as on the album. It's over a year since I've been on stage which is too long a time by far. I want to get out there and strut my stuff again . . . " He began to plan that long awaited return to the stage more seriously once recording was finished – indeed he spent almost the rest of the year getting a group together. Micky Moody signed up almost at once. "Micky and myself were the nucleus. I wanted to build the band around him," Coverdale later explained.

Mick Moody was born in Middlesborough on August 30, 1950 and he spent his formative years in much the same stomping ground as David Coverdale. "Micky's been playing in bands for years," he explained. "When I was 15 he was 16, playing stuff like 'Beck's Boogie' when most people hadn't even heard the record." Moody began his recording career as lead guitarist with Ramline, playing on their début album in 1968. Prior to that his musical upbringing had been the fairly typical round of local groups.

Acquiring his first electric guitar on HP when he was 15, Moody formed a local band called The Roadrunners with bassist Paul Rogers with whom he went to school. Moody's admiration for Chuck Berry and the like, together with his first blast of Eric Clapton didn't square well with his attempts to become an accountant so jacking in his day job, he and Rogers changed the band's name to The Wild Flowers, and decided to travel down to London to make their fortune. Rogers, known to locals as Prickly Will because of his notoriously short temper, switched to lead vocals during the process.

The band starved, though their members all eventually went on to greater things, Rogers with Free and bassist Bruce Thomas as one of Elvis Costello's Attractions. Micky Moody returned to Middlesborough and together with other local musicians formed Tramline who made two albums for Island Records, the second of which saw Colin Hodgkinson and Ron Asprey roped in to help.

The album flopped and the band split, Moody returning to London three months later to join first Mike Cotton, then Zoot Money and then in 1971 Juicy Lucy just after their first album had been issued. They

The promotional poster for Coverdale's second solo album, Northwinds.

Ian Paice, backstage at the first PAL show.

Bassist Neil Murray.

were riding high after the Vertigo smash single 'Who Do You Love' and Moody stayed with them for three albums, getting a taste of the controversy that would later resurface with Whitesnake's record sleeves when objections to both 'Lie Back And Enjoy It' and the follow-up 'Get A Whiff Of This' nearly got the albums withdrawn.

After 'Pieces' the band folded but Moody had an offer to join a new band called Snafu, formed by one-time Procol Harum drummer Bobby Harrison in March of 1973. Harrison (who had given up the drums to concentrate on singing) had begun a solo album earlier that year using Tony Iommi, Deep Purple drummer Ian Paice and Micky Moody. It was during these sessions that the idea for Snafu with Pete Solley on keyboards evolved. They took their name from the initials of a much used soldiers phrase – Situation Normal All Fucked Up – and had a fairly busy two years on the road, taping three albums along the way and only calling it a day early in 1976 when it became clear they weren't going to progress much further.

It was at this point that Coverdale called up Moody and work on the Whitesnake album began. In between working on Coverdale's solo material Moody busied himself with other session work; he was involved with Graham Bonnet's first solo album (this was some time before Bonnet joined Rainbow) and wrote material with Status Quo's Bob Young which was eventually issued in 1977 as the 'Young And Moody' album. Leaning more towards electric country music than Coverdale's material, Moody was able to use up some of the songs which he had offered to David Coverdale, who returned the favour with a song called 'Sunrise To Sunset', which Young and Moody later laid down for their second album. Coverdale wrote it when he was just 15. "Another daft love song, but it's pretty and sincere," he commented at the time.

Coverdale was keen on having a two guitar line-up and Moody agreed as he felt he couldn't fill the role of an up-front guitarist himself. Coverdale thus made approaches to guitarist Mel Galley and his fellow Trapeze cohort, drummer Dave Holland. A long-time admirer of the hard funk style Trapeze had pioneered for so long, as well as their writing, Coverdale saw the chance to bring Mel in and add an edge to his new band. Trapeze in fact disbanded for a time but had reformed with a newly released album which Galley was keen to promote, so he declined the offer. Coverdale's next call was to Bernie Marsden.

Bernie Marsden, born May 7, 1951 in Buckingham, came relatively late to a musical career. It wasn't until the end of the sixties that he finally decided to devote himself full time to rock. His first gig of any real consequence was with UFO, where in November 1972 he replaced Larry Wallis, off to join The Pink Fairies. However, when Bernie missed a show in Germany, Michael Schenker, then with the embryonic Scorpions, filled in and replaced him full time in June 1973.

Bernie went on to join Wild Turkey with former Jethro Tull bassist Glenn Cornick. After that things could only get better and his next move promised much. He teamed up with Cozy Powell, one of the original drummers from the British nailers school. Cozy Powell's Hammer showed promise but they found it hard to shrug off the glitter image Cozy had earned from his chart hits and so in 1975 Marsden teamed up with Babe Ruth after their guitarist and founder member Alan Shacklock left.

Despite the talents of lead vocalist Jenny Haan they were falling apart and Marsden recruited Neil Murray to play bass on their last album. They called it a day in 1976 and Bernie was kicking his heels when a call from Cozy Powell told him of a job going in which he might be interested. This was Paice, Ashton, Lord.

PAL grew out of Jon Lord's friendship with keyboard player Tony Ashton. Back in the early seventies Deep Purple's manager had signed up Ashton, Gardener and Dyke, to be rewarded with a hit single

Jon Lord during PAL days.

Drummer David 'Duck' Dowle.

called 'Resurrection Shuffle'. It was a one-off and several often entertaining but financially unsuccessful albums followed.

Lord was smitten by Ashton's style however and the pair issued an album called 'The First Of The Big Bands' in 1974. It lacked cohesion, put together as it was in such a long drawn out way, and didn't sell well at the time, yet it did establish the heavy rock and blues foundations which Paice, Ashton, Lord were to build on. When Deep Purple split Jon Lord had little hesitation in sinking his earnings into a new band with Ian Paice and Tony Ashton. Nothing was announced publicly but mysterious ads appeared in the music papers during July of 1976: ''British Band requires British Bass Player and Lead Guitarist for formation of new rock band by three established musicians.''

Every bassist and guitarist in the country was alerted. They were still struggling to find a suitable guitarist when Bernie Marsden turned up for a late audition. He never saw the ads in the papers and if it hadn't been for Cozy's call would have missed out altogether. PAL (or Plaice, Haddock and Cod as Coverdale was wont to refer to them) were under pressure from management who were no doubt after a band which could take over from Deep Purple in terms of earning power and popularity. ''We've sunk about £100,000 into this band. With that financial and professional commitment there's no way we're not going to be doing our damnedest to make PAL a success,'' Jon told a reporter during the rehearsals. The album came out to generally good reviews but less than spectacular sales. On top of that a full European tour was ditched leaving just five British dates intact.

Their actual début came opening the BBC's new *Sight And Sound In Concert* series, a dubious honour indeed. The recording was fraught with problems, the band managed to blow up the BBC generators twice. This and the pressure unnerved Ashton considerably and affected his ability to cope with the vocals. Coming

at such an important stage in their career, the TV début did more harm than good. Exactly a week later they opened their tour at Birmingham Odeon and while things were fine musically, Ashton was clearly not up to fronting the band. His style and approach worked in a small club but on-stage in front of a couple of thousand people he failed to come across.

Once the tour was over the group began work on their second album but with backing tracks done Ashton decided he wanted out and they came to a mutual decision to fold. Lord and Paice made further efforts to secure Coverdale's services to rescue the situation but to no avail. They even toyed with the idea of reverting to the Deep Purple name if Coverdale would join. The plan never came to fruition and PAL's guitarist Bernie Marsden was at a loose end.

Coverdale caught one of their shows and called to ask if he wanted to come along and jam. He and Moody seemed to work well together and he was duly enrolled. Auditioning went on, with bassist Chris Stewart next to appear. Micky Moody did a short tour of America with Frankie Miller in August 1977 and met Stewart there. A few days later he called in unable to attend rehearsals. With a drummer to audition, Bernie hit on the idea of getting his friend Neil Murray, who lived close by, to deputise for the occasion.

Neil Murray was born in Edinburgh on August 27, 1950. He is one of those rare bass players who actually played the instrument more or less from the start rather than ending up on bass after failing to make the grade on lead guitar as is often the case, though he had a brief spell on drums in a school band. Neil was inspired, as were many others during the sixties, by the talents of Jack Bruce in Cream and he got his first bass guitar in 1967. His first group of any consequence, which he joined straight from college, was Gilgamesh, one of the Canterbury bands who thrived in the wake of Caravan, Soft Machine and the like.

During 1972 Murray met bassist Clive Chaman

through a mutual friend Bobby Tench. Chaman and Tench were both at that time playing alongside Cozy Powell in Jeff Beck's band and, keen to expand his style, Murray visited Chaman's house over the next couple of years to practise and learn some of Chaman's Motown-influenced style. It was through Chaman that Murray was recommended to Junior Hanson, a would-be Hendrix disciple who was looking to form a band after taping his first album (with Chaman on bass).

That gig lasted through an album called 'Magic Dragon' in 1974 until Junior was busted during a short American club tour. Clive Chaman stepped in again but in the middle of 1974 Chaman wanted time off from Hammer (where he'd gone with Powell) to play with Linda Lewis in London, recommending Neil Murray as a stand-in while he was away and again in 1975 under similar circumstances.

It was here that Neil met Bernie Marsden, the two becoming friends. When Hammer split up, Neil Murray teamed up with their keyboard player Don Airey in Colosseum II. Neil also deputised once more for Clive Chaman, this time backing singer Doris Troy, where he met and played alongside drummer Dave Dowle. Not long afterwards the pair of them auditioned together for Roger Chapman's Streetwalkers. Dowle got the job, Murray didn't.

In July 1976, after being fired from Colosseum along with the singer, Murray joined National Health, a jazz-rock outfit which included some of Neil's friends from Gilgamesh as well as people from Hatfield And The North. "It meant a lot of poverty and getting into areas of being a little too intellectual musically. There was a bit of snobbery as well. I was disillusioned making virtually no money, coupled with the lack of gigs and the overly intellectual nature of the music, which had very little to do with the exciting jazz rock fusion of bands like Weather Report," Neil recalled.

To earn some money Neil Murray took a day job shrink wrapping records for the mighty Virgin Megastore in London. Then on December 5, 1977 he received a call from Bernie Marsden. He explained that they were short of a bassist for the day and would Neil mind helping them audition a drummer? Murray, who lived in Camden Town near to the rehearsal room, agreed. The drummer in question was Neil Potts from Praying Mantis.

Murray enjoyed himself, though he was unimpressed with Potts' style. A couple of days later Chris Stewart told Coverdale he had decided to return to Frankie Miller's band; Neil Murray was asked back. Given his background he might have seemed an unusual choice. However, while Murray enjoys the challenge jazz rock presents he admits to feeling that bands often forsake feeling to pursue technical excellence. Murray preferred to be giving it some stick doing rock. "It's the first time I haven't been thinking in complex musical terms but simply in terms of straight rock bass playing. I'm playing with my heart now, not my head," he explained later. They discussed drummers and Dave Dowle's name came up. When Murray said he had already worked with him, that more or less clinched it.

David Dowle, another Londoner, born on October 20, 1953, was about to be thrown back on the dole as The Streetwalkers disbanded that same month so his audition was timely. He was signed up and

the group began their very first full rehearsals on December 16, 1977.

Coverdale spent his spare evenings checking out bands in London, on the look-out for any likely recruits as they were still short of a keyboard player. Down at the Speakeasy one night he was accosted by a spiky haired individual who asked him who he was. "I'm a boring old fart," came the reply. "And who might you be?" "I'm Sid Vicious," the individual replied. "Well I'm David Ferocious so I suggest you leave before I put your lights out," replied David.

Over Christmas Coverdale decided that the band he'd assembled was working well enough in rehearsal to form the basis of Whitesnake and the line-up was announced in January, though who the Neil Murphy of EMI's album release sheet was, remains a mystery. The second solo album was ready for release and live dates would be arranged to promote it. An organist still eluded them ("Neil is so conservative he suggested Edward Heath for keyboards," Coverdale chuckled, explaining the difficulties they were having) and in the end Brian Johnston was drafted in just in time for the final round of rehearsals in mid-February.

Johnston had been in The Streetwalkers since September 1976, joining not long after Dave Dowle, who suggested offering him the Whitesnake gig. Micky Moody remembered Johnston from the sixties soul bands and wondered at the wisdom of taking him on. "David wanted the organ sound of Jon Lord . . . well very few people get that kind of sound and Brian certainly wasn't one of them. We actually had better players down but they didn't seem to play the organ, so he got the gig." With time fast running out it was a case of Hobson's choice.

'Northwinds' was issued in March 1978 after some considerable trouble over the cover. Originally a design featuring a moody sepia shot of David against a landscape of hills and lakes was worked up to proof stage. It turned out less dramatic than they'd hoped so EMI coughed up for a new piece of artwork, the Hipgnosis influenced moorland cover eventually used. Even then the first print run lost much of the subtlety of the colours so the job was redone for the second printing.

Musically it was a vast improvement on the first album. There was again a mixture of styles and moods but Coverdale's confidence had returned and the performances were in a different league. The quieter tracks like 'Time And Again' and 'Say You Love Me' sounded sincere, while the heavier material delivered without resorting to metal clichés. 'Queen Of Hearts', the excellent 'Only My Soul', still one of his best vocal performances and the out-and-out Purple influenced 'Breakdown' still sound good today, even if the latter did lean a little on the title track from his first solo album. It was decided to issue it as a single. A fast and furious number which told the story of Purple's final demise from David's viewpoint, it was a useful way of putting an end to that part of his career and introducing a new era. "With Purple it wasn't a break-up but a breakdown, there's no way I could write a song about it without sounding like Purple," he said.

IV

February 1978 - October 1978

'BACK TO THE ROOTS' TOUR TO LORD'S ARRIVAL

1978

Previous Page: Jon Lord.

With 'Northwinds' out of the way, Whitesnake started to rehearse their live set. Their gear was set up in an old warehouse, the rather grandly named Halligan And Heap Rehearsal Rooms, near London's Caledonian Road. Here they knocked into shape tracks from the solo albums, together with some standards and a couple of the more suitable Deep Purple tunes. None of the band had been great fans of Purple but the later period where Coverdale's, and to a larger extent Glenn Hughes', black influences came into play had produced a few numbers which lent themselves to Whitesnake's style. Coverdale himself joined the rehearsals between bursts of interviews with the music press.

The tour was organised rather quickly with the aim of both promoting 'Northwinds' and launching the group who, at most of the gigs, were billed as David Coverdale's Whitesnake. "I'd like to drop the name and just use Whitesnake but I'm told that politically it's best to keep my name to the fore," he remarked in the time honoured tradition of solo artists with an illustrious past.

Some promoters simply put The David Coverdale Band on the posters and left it at that. The plan was to get the band on the road in a low-key fashion without resorting to support act status, so they were booked in to clubs and colleges across the country.

In the haste to set it up, gigs were not checked sufficiently and were completely unsuitable for the band – indeed for any live rock show. Small or non-existent stages, pillars obscuring the view and

inadequate power supplies were just a few of the problems. This meant dates were rearranged even as they hit the road, with some of the worst places cancelled altogether. In fairness most were booked unseen over the phone, with the club owners (possibly in an effort to secure the band) exaggerating the merits of their premises. "At one venue the stage turned out to be as big as my office desk," tour manager Ossie Hoppe told one disgruntled fan when complaints about late cancellations reached the music papers.

After pulling out of just such a gig in Nottingham at the Skybird Club, the band made their live début at the Technical College in Lincoln on March 3, 1978, with Brian Johnston still part of the crew.

Despite the venue problems it was an excellent tour, as anyone who packed into the tiny clubs to see them will testify. Coverdale himself was pissed off at having to abort some shows. "They haven't had the capacity to get my equipment in . . . not my genitals, but stuff like lights and things. One concert we did Micky was in the middle of a guitar solo and a guy leaned over and asked him what strings he was using." Another problem was the over-18 only age limit which some clubs enforced quite strictly, though the band did sneak a few fans in via stage doors when nobody was looking.

For Coverdale one of the emotional highpoints was a show at The Coatham Bowl in Redcar, just a few miles from his home town. "The atmosphere was fantastic," one fan told a local reporter afterwards. "The place

Back To The Roots tour, Wolverhampton, March 1978.

Whitesnake, May 1978. *(L–R)* Dowell, Moody, Coverdale, Murray. *(Front)* Solley and Marsden.

was crammed. People had to stand on chairs and tables to get a glimpse of the band.'' The local recreation department who organised the gig were also enthusiastic, adding, ''If he ever comes back this way we will certainly be trying to get him at the Bowl.'' Coverdale was in two minds, confiding to a friend that there seemed to be more people backstage than out front, most of whom hadn't wanted to know him when he'd lived there.

Whitesnake's London début came at the Music Machine in Camden, now The Camden Palace, where they managed to set a new attendance record for the venue. As is often the case with shows in London, nerves got the better of the band. Despite most musicians professed couldn't-care-less attitude about the press, it can't be easy watching pencils scribbling away (and the bar filling up).

At Manchester's, 'No membership, come as you are', den of hard rock iniquity, the Rafters Club, punk was ruling the day, with Generation X, The Saints and The Pleasers just a few of the acts booked the same week as Whitesnake. The audience grew slowly until by 11pm it was like the black hole of Calcutta down there and sneaking off with bar stools was the only way to get a decent view, unless you were prepared (like one over-enthusiastic fan) to climb into the rafters themselves.

The band came on and delivered. There were rough edges but the overall power was incredible, even more so in such a tiny venue. They concentrated on the first album and while it sounded much better for tightening up, it was a shame some of the better material from 'Northwinds' was never heard on-stage. Instead they fell back on standards, including 'Rock Me Baby' and 'Ain't

No Love In The Heart Of The City', which became a stage favourite for many years having been used for auditioning musicians the previous year. To show he hadn't forgotten the good times in Purple, they threw in 'Lady Double Dealer', an excellent version of 'Lady Luck' (which showed just how good the later Purple songs could have been live) and 'Mistreated', the classic blues track he and Blackmore made so much their own when they taped it back in 1973. ''I never wrote that song, I just busked along 'cause I was scared and lonely, me and Blackmore . . . those are the words you'll hear on the album,'' he reminisced during the tour.

'Breakdown' closed the show, sung with ferocity and as a group they rocked out with feeling, the twin guitar sound not unlike Wishbone Ash's better days. It was an exhilarating show. The tour ended in Plymouth at the Castaways Club on March 29.

After so long away from the rigours of touring, Coverdale's voice began to give out and the last two concerts had to be cancelled. It was also agreed among the others that Brian Johnston wasn't fitting in. During that last show the band were steaming away and Coverdale, finishing a verse prior to the keyboard solo, turned and in his aggressive rock and roll fashion yelled ''Yeeaahh,'' cueing Johnston in. ''He ducked down and hid behind the organ,'' Micky Moody recalled, laughing at the memory. ''He thought David was going to hit him. He used to wear those old fashioned satin shirts with lettuce leaves down the front. He was definitely the wrong man.''

At Moody's suggestion they contacted Pete Solley who had been with him in Snafu, as well as in Paladin and Procol Harum. Solley was then getting into

David Coverdale & Whitesnake in action at Manchester and in London, 1978 . . .

production work and wasn't keen to go on the road, though he agreed to help out in the studio on a session basis. It was decided that before getting down to an album, Whitesnake would issue an EP as a way of getting some up to date material out as quickly as possible. After a couple of days' rehearsal Whitesnake went straight into the Central Studios in London to rattle off four tracks, written prior to the tour, Coverdale again launching out on a series of local radio interviews once the recording was over. They stuck in a couple more live gigs too and the audience in Reading on April 25 saw Pete Solley playing keyboards on-stage with the band for the first time.

In May, while the finishing touches to the EP package were made, the band trooped down to Shepperton Studios to make a promo film to go with it. The 'Snakebite' EP hit the stores at the front end of June, resplendent in a picture bag, white vinyl and special labels – promotional luxuries still fairly unusual in the UK at that time. One paper got The Rich Kids' Midge Ure to review the week's releases. "I hate groups that release records on coloured vinyl," was the limit of his critical powers, while his accomplice said simply: "I hate records like this and I hate David Coverdale."

The short 'Snakebite' film went out the same month as a support feature to David Hamilton's soft porn movie *Bilitis*. The dawn of the video age had still not quite broken and with TV a fairly closed shop, this was about the only way it could be seen in Britain. Coverdale's brush with the film industry led to a few offers, including a part in an upcoming Jackie Collins movie titled *The World Is Full Of Married Men*, a follow-up to *The Stud*. He was unable to fit it in to his schedule; likewise some music he wrote for a film called *Lipstick* never got beyond the writing stage.

Musically the EP sounds somewhat primitive these days but it did include two of the tracks aired during the tour: 'Ain't No Love In The Heart Of The City', the blues standard which had been going down well and 'Steal Away', which was one of the live highlights already. Both lacked the intensity of the stage versions, a problem which would dog the band for some time to

come. Of the other tracks, 'Come On' marked Bernie Marsden's writing début in the band. "There was this spark, we sat down and wrote a song together the first afternoon which eventually became 'Come On'."

The plug track 'Bloody Mary' got a fair amount of airplay too, enough to earn slots on both *Top Of The Pops* and a much livelier appearance on the opposition network's excellent but short lived *Revolver* show. Neil Murray recalled the inept technicians in the studio for the latter, who refused to listen to Bernie Marsden's

. . . and filming the Snakebite promo.

fears that they were recording the sound wrong. They set off home and took a break in a service station where anxious people from the TV station, who had been trying every café on the route home, finally caught up with them to explain that the guitars hadn't come out and could they come back and redo it? In Europe the four EP tracks were combined with four songs from 'Northwinds' to create an album titled 'Snakebite'.

Resplendent in a collection of live photos from the March tour, its appearance back home as an import caused confusion among fans. It also became their very first American release when United Artists, who had turned David Coverdale down as a solo artist the previous year, took up an option on it. They decided that the cover looked too much like a live album and did a hasty rework before putting it out. The record reportedly sold no more than 1,000 copies in total when it was issued in October of that year.

Whitesnake returned to Central Studios in May and June to lay down their first proper album, Coverdale adding the vocals at the end of June. There were plans to go out as the support act on UFO's nationwide tour after the recording but the feedback after the club tour was such that it looked more promising to get the album out and headline to support it later in the year. "David was confident we could fill these places and he was right," Micky Moody observed. On top of this they also did their first show on foreign soil at Alkmaar in Holland. Sessions over, the band did an unhappy half hour on the BBC Radio *In Concert* series. Coverdale, cheesed off by the attitudes he encountered there, hit the bottle a little too heavily prior to going on — unusually too, he generally kept celebrating until after the shows (or on the bus, or at the hotel) and these days claims to have knocked it on the head completely.

They also did their first major London show at the Lyceum, one of the few with Solley as part of the band. There was some aggro because the promoters mismatched Whitesnake with two punk bands as support and rival factions among the crowd caused a ruck during the evening.

On the keyboard front Coverdale still wasn't happy. Hearing that Ian Gillan was about to disband his group he made enquiries about Colin Towns and some of the band went along to see them at the Music Machine in London but nothing came of it. He also gave Jon Lord another bell. The album was finished when Jon Lord finally made his mind up and decided to accept Coverdale's offer.

Jon Lord, born in Leicester on July 9, 1941, had been kicking about in the music business since the early sixties, spending several years with The Artwoods and

London's Lyceum Theatre, July 1978.

HARVEY GOLDSMITH ENTERTAINMENTS PRESENT

DAVID COVERDALE'S WHITESNAKE
+ DEAD FINGERS TALK
+ SUPPORT
+ D.J. ANDY DUNKLEY

THE LYCEUM   SUNDAY 9th JULY
DOORS OPEN 7.15   SHOW STARTS 8.00
TICKETS: 1·75 IN ADVANCE   2·00 ON THE DOOR   Box Office 836 3715
AND HARVEY GOLDSMITH BOX OFFICE AT CHAPPELS 50 NEW BOND ST. TEL. 629 3453

supplementing his income with session work. During
one session he met bassist Nick Simper and the
foundations of Deep Purple were laid.

When they split in 1976 he formed PAL. By May of
1978, following their demise, Ian Paice and Jon Lord
were busy forming a group to back Maggie Bell,
formerly of Stone The Crows. The line-up was
announced in June and a special celebratory come-back
show was set for July 16. Joining Lord and Paice were
Paul Martinez, Andy Mackay from Roxy Music and
Geoff Whitehorn from Crawler on guitar. Apart from
Whitehorn, the line-up was supposed to be permanent,
with plans to record an album after the concert. In the
event, only two tracks got done and these were never
released. Finance was not forthcoming and the project
floundered.

Jon had felt misgivings about it in any case.
"We were introduced as The Maggie Bell Band. I began
to feel my accumulated kudos melting away," –
understandable after a decade at the top. Coverdale had
already thought about Jon joining Whitesnake early in
1978. "Jon and I went through a weird period at one
time and neither of us really understands why. I think it
was just that we had a lot of trouble with the last six
months of Purple," he said later. The two met up again
in court that year where they were involved in a case

brought by the widow of Ron Quinton, a former Deep
Purple roadie who died on the road in America.

During the case, Lord simply scribbled a brief note
passed to David which said, "Can I be of help?" He was
also in demand elsewhere; as well as an offer of a job
with Ritchie Blackmore's Raincoat (as Whitesnake were
often to refer to Blackmore's band), he lived near Bad
Company guitarist Mick Ralphs who was pushing for
Jon to be brought in as their keyboard player. In the end
Paul Rogers decided against expanding the band and Jon
was at a loose end once more. He was still wary about
Whitesnake, fearing that David had simply gone and
taken the Deep Purple style over into a new outfit.
Micky Moody recalled the period . . .

"David called him a few times and Jon had
hummed and ha'd. The thing that swayed him was the
'Snakebite' EP. Jon always maintained that the reason
he joined was because it was blues based and Jon loves
the blues. When he heard the EP and the slide guitar
and the Bloody Marys he said he wanted in." So when
Coverdale called him again towards the end of the year,
Jon didn't need long to think about it. The day after he
joined he was off into the studio. Solley's contributions
were wiped and Lord overdubbed the keyboards.
"You should have heard him, the studio walls shook,"
Coverdale enthused later. "There was so much emotion
on the tracks that it almost felt as though I was playing
with the band, not sitting in a studio on my own with
headphones on," Jon reported later.

The group began several weeks of rehearsals and the
build up to the tour started. News of his arrival was
made public early in August, along with plans for a full
scale British tour and their first album, provisionally
titled 'Hit And Run'.

CHAPTER V

October 1978
- December 1979

'TROUBLE' LP/TOUR
TO 'LOVEHUNTER'

'Trouble', as the album was eventually titled, reached the stores in October in time for the British tour, its textured cover a simple affair with a small coiled snake graphic in the centre. Musically, like the sleeve, the album was rather two dimensional and by the time they hit the road the band had improved so much so that the album versions of most tracks suffered in comparison. There was an excess of material, as Dave Dowle explained. ''We decided at the start that we wanted a heavy album, we left off a lot of ballady things so we could come out with a really hard hitting album. The only pity was that Jon joined the band after the basic recordings and had to add his parts later. He has got that something special which can drive a band along as well as just supplying the keyboards.''

The album isn't especially dated musically because the band's basic style wasn't one which was particularly fashionable, yet it showed they had a way to go before they began to add anything new to the blues/rock field rather than come across as adequate but unmemorable Bad Company or Free clones. Vocally Coverdale sounded as if he'd meant it on his previous solo album but here the performance often sounds hurried and uninspired. The production has a nice rough edge to it, something the band was keen not to lose by taking too long in the studio, while instrumentally the performances are generally good. Bernie Marsden's influence is obvious on two numbers where he brought in his jazz rock style, though Coverdale doesn't sound at ease trying to sing over them.

Jon Lord's contributions are barely audible and as if to make sure you know he's there the final organ chords of several numbers are drawn out long after the track has faded. He does get to do his best sixties Keith Emerson pastiche on the album's instrumental 'Belgian Tom's Hat Trick', a jazzy shuffle which became an on-stage solo vehicle. 'Don't Mess With Me' ended the album and despite the awkward changes of tempo and the remarkable resemblance of the riff to that on Rainbow's 'Light In The Black', is a more distinctively Whitesnake track. Curiously the two numbers which still seem to have something to offer today are an interesting version of The Beatles' 'Day Tripper' and the album's opening cut, 'Take Me With You' – always start with your best shot – a guitar based rocker featuring some excellent bass lines from Neil Murray. Only lightweight drumming lets it down; indeed Dowle only sounds at home on the jazzier tracks where he has the freedom to experiment.

Not the world's most auspicious first album then. It did get an American release, hot on the heels of 'Snakebite' though once again United Artists took one look at the British cover and ordered their art department to come up with something more attractive. Featuring an airbrushed white snake uncoiling from a purple egg (symbolic huh?), EMI were impressed enough to reissue the album using the American cover art a couple of years later.

The new line-up with Jon Lord made their début on TV in Germany plugging 'Bloody Mary', returning to

Whitesnake as they began their British tour, Autumn 1978. *(L–R)* Murray, Marsden, Coverdale, Moody, Lord and Dowell.

Britain to perform two tracks on the *Old Grey Whistle Test*, an often infuriating TV music show with a budget so tight they resorted to filling half their air time with album tracks sequenced to cheapo animations. Nevertheless it was one of the few programmes which would venture outside the realms of the top 30 charts. "Before we got going the producer came over and said, 'Do us a favour lads, can you turn it down?' otherwise the cameramen were going to walk out," recalled Coverdale of the show. The group managed to plug the single 'Lie Down' and the LP title track too, though sadly the warm-up number, a version of the Tom Jones classic 'It's Not Unusual' was not broadcast for posterity.

The tour proper kicked off up in Newcastle. It was an important outing given the decision to go out headlining and they had also dropped the David Coverdale monicker on the album and tour adverts as promised the year before. Backstage Coverdale paced up and down as the support group, Magnum (with Richard Bailey on keyboards), went through their paces. "Why do I die a thousand deaths like this before I go on?" he remarked to a reporter covering the opening shows.

In another room Marsden and Moody were warming up, Jon Lord likening it to "a bar in South Carolina in there" as the two boogied away. Two hours later the dressing room atmosphere was transformed, the place humming as the band wound down from a more than successful live début. Coverdale, reduced to tears, relived some of the highlights, groping for words to try and explain the experience.

At one point in the show the whole crowd had taken over 'Ain't No Love In The Heart Of The City'. "It wasn't planned. I just had this feeling and told the guys to bottle it. How can you talk about that? Sometimes it actually transcends sex," Coverdale said. Jon Lord was on hand as ever to bring him back to earth. "You old tart, this will all sound very silly." Yet even a hardened pro like him had to admit to being well pleased with events. "I haven't been this happy for three years, not since before Ritchie left Purple. It was absolutely right. I even kissed Micky Moody, I must be mad." Later he even proposed marriage to David, who wisely asked for time to think it over.

Overall the tour exceeded expectations, barring niggles in Edinburgh when Coverdale had problems with a mike stand that was too short, ("Who's been getting gear off Ronnie Dio?" he griped at a roadie off-stage), a bomb scare at Cardiff, a not uncommon occurrence at gigs in the late seventies, and some dodgy planning which saw Ian Gillan débuting his revamped band around Britain the same month, in a manner similar to the back to the roots style adopted by Coverdale earlier in the year.

The pair met up on the local radio circuit and talked vaguely about doing an album of rock and roll covers together. Nothing ever came of it . . . by chucking out time they'd probably forgotten all about it.

In Manchester the two gigs clashed, Ian playing at the Mayflower Club and Whitesnake headlining at the Ardwick Apollo, an unusually grim example of the cinema builders art left high and dry by Manchester Corporation's grandiose town planning schemes. For a first major tour the show was certainly promising.

Launching into Ain't No Love on the band's first major UK tour.

Marsden & Moody trade licks on Belgian Tom.

Reading 1979. *Top:* Jon Lord. *Middle:* David Coverdale. *Bottom:* Neil Murray.

Despite the expectations of some, Whitesnake refused to deliver a straight head-banging set from start to finish; the material varied throughout and the set was all the better for that.

On the other hand Coverdale decided against doing the quieter songs from the solo albums which was a pity as vocally he was in good form. He'd also lost some of the arrogance which had been evident with Purple and was obviously happy to be doing proper gigs again. The set concentrated on the 'Trouble' album and the EP, tracks like 'Steal Away', which really began to work well live, 'Come On', 'Ain't No Love In The Heart Of The City', 'Lie Down', 'Take Me With You' and 'Belgian Tom's Hat Trick'. To a certain extent the band allowed solos to break up the show's momentum at times and Lord fell back on snippets of old Purple tunes during his solo, a fatal move.

The band still did 'Mistreated' and also introduced 'Might Just Take Your Life', likewise from the 'Burn' album, mainly because it was an organ based number which allowed Jon to shine. On the whole Lord seemed happy to be back on the road, free of the problems which had dogged PAL. He played better than he'd done in years, selflessly too, never upstaging any of the band, except perhaps when he received the loudest applause during band introductions. Coverdale did his best Plant impersonations for 'Rock Me Babe', the first encore, before they blasted out on 'Breakdown'.

If the album was a disappointment then the live shows more than made up for it, a trait which was to mark the band's career for some time yet. The Apollo show was taped using the Island Mobile. Whitesnake was working so well on-stage that they decided to record the odd gig with a view to putting out a 12-inch single. They were completely at a loss as to how to get air-play. A plan to issue their version of 'Day Tripper' was abandoned, even though the band arranged a break in the middle of the tour to make a video for it. The German record company went ahead with it but here they felt issuing it would be pouring money down the drain.

The tour was well attended, despite the fact that most of the music press (with the exception of *Sounds*) ignored anything that didn't fit their concept of new wave or punk. Away from the fickle tastes of the press, word slowly passed among rock fans, keen to see any band brave enough to work in such an unfashionable genre. There were many who remembered Coverdale from Deep Purple and who were curious to see what his new outfit was all about, especially now Jon was in the band.

The tour culminated in a show at the Hammersmith Odeon in London, a venue which over the next few years was to become Whitesnake's unofficial home and once again the gig was taped. The band took December off at the end of a busy year, though Marsden and Coverdale made it to Liverpool to help judge the annual Battle Of The Bands contest. That same month down in a rehearsal room in London, guitarist Robin Trower was running through his new band – with Jim Dewer on bass, Paul Rodgers on vocals and Ian Paice on drums. Paicey was just helping out, as Trower had high hopes of recruiting Aynsley Dunbar.

In fact the line-up never progressed beyond these few rehearsals; Ian says Trower was still too laid back for him to feel he was able to contribute much but he was itching for something more positive to do. After Christmas it was time for Whitesnake to consider the rest of Europe, though the first chore was to overdub the live tape from Hammersmith which was being cleaned up for release.

Whitesnake secured a tour of Germany in February supporting Nazareth which enabled Dan McCafferty to get his own back on Jon Lord for the practical jokes he'd endured several years before when Nazareth had supported Purple in the States, and Lord found his room liberally scented with stink-bombs and his suitcase glued shut. Though their sense of fun was still strong, musically Nazareth's day was nearly over by 1979. The success of singles like 'Broken Down Angel' and 'This Flight Tonight' no longer meant much and the tour didn't really do Whitesnake much good. Halls were often only half full and a fair proportion of those who did turn up had only gone for Whitesnake anyway. Back in Blighty they headlined the Hammersmith Odeon for the second time in March.

The gig was a one-off, all proceeds being donated to the Gunner Nilsson Charity, Nilsson being a Swedish racing driver who died of cancer the year before. As well as the band, all the lighting and ancillary services were donated free of charge. The band were improving all the time, causing at least one reviewer to drastically alter his opinion of them. "Last November I wasn't particularly impressed, but this time they delivered an excellent set of tight aggressive rock. The band were dragged back for not one but three encores."

It is interesting to read old press cuttings and see how many reviewers managed to write disparaging reviews of the band and their audience but who now make their livings writing for magazines that cater for those very people. Back stage among the usual crowd of liggers, Ian Paice turned up full of enthusiasm for the way the band had developed. This was the third time he'd seen them and he was becoming quite a fan.

EMI timed the new single for the same month, backing the album track with a live recording taken

Neil Murray.

Bernie Marsden queues for the phone, Germany 1979.

Ian Paice.

Micky Moody models his t-shirt collection, 1978 & 1979.

from the previous year's Hammersmith show, though sales weren't exactly sparkling. The lack of any sort of special sleeve for this and the next few singles didn't help the problem. Vague plans existed for an eight-week American tour but this was abandoned. Instead they flew out in early April to headline in Paris and then played a few Spanish gigs, where orderly chaos seemed to be the order of the day – at one show a power failure was rectified with a new fuse, only to go off again soon after. Backstage they found a Spanish electrician had taken out the fuse again to check it. They gave up because of the conditions in Barcelona, slipped in a TV show in Madrid instead and returned home to begin recording work on their next album at Clearwell Castle in Gloucester, familiar territory for both Coverdale and Lord who had worked there on three albums with Deep Purple.

Micky Moody found time to do an album for Roger Chapman and also finished his second Young/Moody LP although his record company were more interested in Silver Convention at the time and declined to release it. Guitarist Bernie Marsden was also jotting down ideas for a solo album. When not busy recording, he and Moody managed to keep everyone on their toes with plenty of elaborate hauntings and other practical jokes. The sessions went well and all the backing tracks were laid down in under two weeks. Within the band however, problems arose with Dave Dowle who wasn't fitting in musically or socially. ''He'd been made to feel not part of it during the recording, he was ill for a few days and people wouldn't go and talk to him or anything so the rot was setting in,'' Neil recalled. Dowle was really more into a jazzier style of playing which hadn't really suited Whitesnake, as a listen to the live album would confirm.

Nevertheless he was still with the band as they broke off recordings for a much lengthier German tour which took up the whole of June. It was even less successful than the supporting tour in February, the band were unable to generate as much interest as they

had back home and the tour almost came to an early finish when Coverdale misjudged an airborne mike stand which luckily resulted in nothing more serious than a cut head. With local bands brought in to support, Whitesnake only drew modest crowds and debated whether to pull out or not. In the end it was agreed to see it out in view of the festival dates at the end of the tour. Matters also came to a head with regards to Dave Dowle, who, demoralised after the album recordings, approached the live shows somewhat less than enthusiastically.

''Whitesnake was getting to be like a Spanish hotel; it looked good from the outside but the foundations were a bit shaky,'' Coverdale quipped. After a few shows they discussed who they might approach as a replacement. Neil Murray threw in the idea of Tommy Aldridge, then with Pat Travers but the others were unfamiliar with his work and the choice came down to two main candidates. Coverdale was hot for Cozy Powell and Marsden, who was an old mate, felt likewise.

Powell was by then nearing the end of his tether in Rainbow and he was contacted but declined the offer. Second on the list was Ian Paice, favoured by Moody, Murray and Lord, who phoned him up and offered him the job. Paice accepted. In fact he'd just begun to think about forming a band himself and contacted Geoff Whitehorn from Crawler as well as Colin Towns, though things had not progressed very far when the Whitesnake offer came up. Prior to that, after the Maggie Bell scenario collapsed, Paice retreated to his country house to collect his thoughts. He, like Lord, didn't especially fancy going back to the beginning and starting from scratch with a new group, nor did he relish the prospect of filling a vacancy in an existing group where he would make precious little musical contribution. Again, like Lord, he had checked Whitesnake out and his reaction was very much the same.

Backstage after one show, once he'd helped himself

to the refreshments, he relaxed enough to compliment Coverdale on his achievements, adding that he thought the band were even better than Purple and that he wished to fuck he was in. His wish was now granted. "Paicey's a guvnor drummer, one of the boss drummers," Coverdale explained about his arrival in the group. The German tour finished with the aforementioned festivals. At Aschaffenburg they headlined over a motley collection of bands including Motorhead, yet the following day they were way down on a bill dominated by Dire Straits and headlined by Barclay James Harvest, a band still very popular in Europe even though they have been out of favour in their home country for over a decade.

Back home Whitesnake's autumn tour was announced in the papers, as the trend towards longer

and longer lead in time for tours continued (spurred on no doubt by the realisation that having ticket receipts earning interest in the bank could be very lucrative). The band arrived home in early July, Dave Dowlc was given the Spanish Archer and Ian Paice was duly enrolled into the honourable order of Whitesnake. He slotted in almost straight away and was able to reflect on his predecessor. "His influences were coming through too much. There's a time to be flash but this band isn't it." They celebrated by packing out Central Recorders in London to help Bernie Marsden tape his solo album, Ian sharing the drum chores with Simon Phillips and . . . Cozy Powell.

In the end Marsden's album was released only in Japan and it was almost a year before he could find a label willing to issue it in Britain. Ian Paice had a week

Coverdale demonstrates the tour coach facilities, October 1979 UK tour.

of rehearsal with the band before making his live début at the Bilzen festival in Holland in mid-August, followed closely by Whitesnake's first appearance at the annual Reading Rock And Blues Festival in Britain. While they took second billing to Peter Gabriel on the last day (though they actually went on after him), their style perhaps reflected the festival's title more than many; the event's all-out metal frenzy was still a year or two away.

If Paice's arrival was good news for Whitesnake, the addition of yet another former Deep Purple star was the cue for the press to begin a rather idiotic series of digs at the band. The fact that Whitesnake's style and approach was very different from Purple passed most of them by. What attracted Lord initially to the band was the very fact that Coverdale hadn't gone out and styled his band after Purple and Ian Paice felt likewise, indeed he'd turned down an approach from Ian Gillan not long before simply because he'd felt Ian was harking back to his Deep Purple days too much (we'll argue about that another day).

Bernie Marsden explained that Paice's arrival was simply not part of any, "Dick Pimple reunion master-plan," but simply a case of musical differences between the band and Dowle. It didn't stop the rumours. When these stories did have substance to them it was usually because manager John Coletta was busy wheeling and dealing hoping to make the relevant people an offer

they couldn't refuse, including one whereby the Spanish Tourist Authority would cough up a six figure sum to get Purple to do a one-off in a resort, the Spaniards making their money back selling special all-in trips to the event.

The new album 'Lovehunter' was issued the following month. Unlike the keyboards on 'Trouble', it wasn't really feasible to overdub drums so the tracks were unchanged. It was thus the first Whitesnake album to go out with a different line-up to that actually in the band at the time of release; it wouldn't be the last. The benefits of a year together as a band showed in the first few bars of a curiously low-key opener called 'Long Way From Home'. The sound balance was better and clearer without being over produced, Coverdale was singing better and the keyboards, growling away in the mix, were also a major contribution to the new sound. Lord even sneaked his 'Highway Star' runs into 'Mean Business'.

Overall though, the group were beginning to break free of the influences which had been all too obvious on 'Trouble' and forge a style of their own which, if it wasn't 100 per cent original, was at least a change from a lot of stuff that was around at the time. This was apparent on 'Walking In The Shadow Of The Blues', a classic romp that typified the band's new-found confidence and direction. Even the less memorable tracks were well polished and the band were willing to

Reading Festival 1979.

Argentina they went to the trouble of fitting the woman with some dubious chain bikini which served only to make things worse. If Coletta hoped to shift more albums with his choice of cover art, the ploy failed dismally in the States where the band made tentative steps in September, preceded by an 'off to conquer America' warm-up in Redcar, supported by Saxon.

The US visit was limited to a few promotional interviews to plug the new album and just one live concert at the UCLA Royce Hall in Los Angeles. "That was it. We were all geared up for touring later in the year, probably with Aerosmith, and United Artists said no, they'd spent all the money they wanted to on this trip," Neil Murray explained. Small wonder that the album disappeared without trace. If America wasn't ready for them just yet the story back home was quite different. The band set out on a month-long tour of Britain through October and November with many of the shows completely sold out. David Coverdale could appreciate the situation. "We've got as far as we have done, which is by no means as far as we need to pay for the group, with absolutely no help from the media at all. It's been purely the responsibility of the people who have seen us in concert. We owe everything that Whitesnake has at the moment to our audiences."

Certainly Radio One went out of its way to ignore the single, TV likewise, the video didn't secure a single screening. On stage earlier tours paled into insignificance. While Paice's drum roadie might have cursed left handed drummers every time they tried to set up the kit, his addition to the line-up brought them that missing spark, while his energy and enthusiasm was infectious. With Marsden and Moody refreshingly free of the normal guitar egos, more attention fell on the rhythm department and it wasn't found lacking.

With such a backing, Coverdale was driven to even greater efforts and as he stood exhausted at the end of 'Mistreated', sweating and grasping at the mike stand, bathed in a single white light, few could deny he'd delivered. If he was worn out by the end of the show, the audience were drained as well – barely able to twitch let alone stomp after such a long set. Despite their efforts, the group still found time to let the fans backstage for autographs and a chat, only Ian Paice being absent, zipping home most nights in his Porsche ("If I don't me missis will kill me").

With the exhaustive and exhausting tour over, there was time for a few weeks off before they started work on the next album during December. Ridge Farm Studio, a sixteenth century building in the heart of the Surrey countryside, was not the easiest place in which to get down to work but they devoted plenty of time to this one, mindful of the fact that they had come away on earlier occasions feeling they had achieved only a certain percentage of what they actually hoped to do in the studio.

"We tried last time and set up in a huge crypt in Clearwell Castle; in there it sounded ambient and live but it didn't transfer to tape," Coverdale told a reporter. "I'm very interested working with Ian again because he was instrumental in the production of the sound of Deep Purple. We'll not only have the bonus of his drumming but him behind the desk as well, because he knows exactly what I want." Ian had helped out on several of Purple's records and done some production

tackle less out-and-out heavy material this time round.

If the music was good, the sleeve was less so, a slick airbrushed illustration of a style much favoured by pornographic magazines, showing a naked woman astride a rather vicious looking snake. There were many complaints that this was merely another example of exploitation. "Maybe we have done a wrong un," Bernie mused, "I don't know." Coverdale himself was unable to see what all the fuss was about, sure in the knowledge that most people knew about the roots of rock and roll. That's not to say it can't be taken to a higher level, but that as far as he was concerned Whitesnake were not about to do so. "The media spends far too much time agonising. They believe they're in touch with the street and they ain't. They think the street is getting pissed at lunchtime with Steve Harley."

In reality the person behind the sleeve was hiding back at the record company offices; step forward Whitesnake manager John Coletta, who obviously subscribed to the view that any publicity is good publicity. Coincidentally the month the album came out, I happened to see a poster advertising an exhibition of old engravings, the featured drawing showing a woman astride a snake. That's art though.

In America, where the system can be even more hypocritical, the cover went out with a large sticker masking the supposedly offending area while in

In full flight, Lovehunter tour 1979.

work outside the band with Elf and Silverhead.

Whitesnake were having problems getting a good sound on album, as people familiar with their recent work will probably notice if they compare today's immense production jobs with the very basic sound on earlier material. To a large extent they were experimenting as they went along. Neil Murray confesses to hardly playing the early albums at all now. "Martin could have been a lot more critical of the performances, he wasn't really standing back and criticising anything to do with the songs, it was just get a good sound and then mix it. Maybe with another producer the results would have been a bit more long lasting, they sound a bit dated to me now." Another Whitesnake spin-off also reached the stores towards the end of the year, a version of 'We Wish You Well' from 'Lovehunter' done by a band called Company.

While no mention of it was made on the disc, the single actually featured several members of Whitesnake – Lord, Murray and Marsden. Jon Lord and Ian Paice

saw the year out jamming with members of Bad Company under the name Pishill Artists; not, as we suspected a crude monicker, the place actually exists, though you pronounce it Pies Hill. Boz Burrell, Simon Kirke and Mick Ralphs along with near neighbour George Harrison gave numbers like 'Smokestack Lightning' and 'Watermelon Man' a good work out. Ian Paice even had the jam taped but don't hold your breath waiting for it to hit the stores.

Over in America United Artists were told that their services (if you could call them that) were no longer required and the band signed instead to Mirage, part of the Atlantic conglomerate. "UA (America) pressed an amazing 11,000 copies of the last album. We do better than that in fucking Middlesborough," griped Coverdale. If they were hoping for better things with Mirage, Whitesnake were to be disappointed.

C H A P T E R   VI

1980

READY AN' WILLING

Previous Page: Japanese tour 1980, advert and ticket.

Whitesnake looked forward during 1980 to reaping the rewards of two years' hard work. They spent two weeks in early February at Central in London putting the finishing touches to the new album, 'Ready An' Willing'. Coverdale then flew home to Germany where he crossed paths with Rainbow, finishing the German leg of a long European tour.

Versions of events differ according to whoever is telling the tale but it seems Blackmore made a grab at Coverdale's hair, who retaliated by turning round to chin the guy and the two of them ended up on the floor, though no punches were landed. Further antics back at the hotel involving jammed door bells and scribbled demonic notes on doors didn't exactly endear the man in black to the Whitesnake vocalist, probably more concerned about how it affected his wife who perhaps wasn't quite so well versed in Blackmore's after hours pranks as he was. The papers had a field day, managing to tie it all in with more harping on about a Deep Purple reunion, despite efforts on behalf of all the relevant people to lay it to rest. ''It would just destroy two and a half years' very hard work,'' Jon pointed out.

Coverdale was more pragmatic. ''There should be some good fights on-stage.'' The pros and cons of having three fifths of Deep Purple in the group did get to the others at times, though they were all on the same wage in Whitesnake at that period. Both Lord and Paice were used to the luxuries of life and their ability to indulge in some of the flashier aspects of consumer durables did irritate at times; even Coverdale was generally against any ostentatious displays while on the road. As Neil Murray said, they were never made to feel bad about it and it also had some advantages. ''It meant that because they wouldn't stand for going in the back of a Ford Transit. If something wasn't done properly, then they weren't going to do it and that rubbed off on everybody else so we all got decent hotels and a decent standard of touring.''

While Coverdale was home in Germany, there was time for a brief rest prior to upcoming tour commitments while the album was prepared for the shops. Micky Moody obviously couldn't wait and joined Quo man John Coghlan's spare time band Diesel for a few dates in March along with Neil Murray, who wanted to work in his hand again after an operation to free a trapped tendon. Before the new studio set arrived, 'Live At Hammersmith' was issued in Japan. Whitesnake had already decided against releasing it in the UK, realising that it would be better to issue something based on more recent tapes than resort to a two-year-old recording done when the band had only been together for eight months.

In Japan, however, five years had passed since Coverdale had last been there and it was felt that the release of a live album would boost interest in the group before they toured there in April. Once the set was out, copies soon began to appear as imports in Europe where the group had already established a strong following; indeed it rapidly became the number one imported album of that year. It was a messy situation which didn't help a band who had endeavoured to give their supporters a fair deal as much as they could.

Devoted fans eager for new material even forced imports of Bernie Marsden's first solo album issued in Japan at the same time; dedicated Coverdale followers

realised he'd helped co-write some tracks under the name Bobby Dazzler. Just before they left for that Japanese tour, Whitesnake (supported by Saxon) headlined a show at London's Rainbow Theatre as part of a special week of concerts celebrating the venue's fiftieth year as a centre of entertainment. A fraught show, Judas Priest managed to overload the PA the night before so the sound wasn't all it ought to have been. Still, Whitesnake had the honour of being the first of the gigs to sell out, not bad considering the competition from The Jam, The Stranglers and Judas Priest.

While the band were busy in Japan, the first fruits of the latest recording sessions were available to fans in Britain and elsewhere with the release of 'Fool For Your Loving'.

The care taken over the sessions had been worthwhile. For the first time the power which had only been hinted at on earlier sets was captured on vinyl; everything about the track was somehow just right. It cut through all the rubbish that had been printed about the band and climbed the UK charts. The talk now was of a 'heavy metal revival' and even if the press felt they had to set up a category before it was safe to start talking about it, they were at least beginning to lower the blinkers. As well as coverage in the papers, even rags like *Jackie* began to home in on the group, while the ultimate accolade came with *Smash Hits* printing the words to the hit song.

Sales of the single were boosted with a nifty (and unique) cover which featured graphics printed in luminous ink. For once the band's timing was perfect. They returned from Japan (a marathon 26-hour plane trip) to find the excellent 'Fool For Your Loving' video (a classy looking affair shot during the Rainbow gig's soundcheck, with audience footage from the concert itself mixed in, on *Top Of The Pops* and the single just outside the Top 10 best sellers.

The UK tour in June tied in with 'Ready An' Willing' and with the benefit of a hit single the group were set to take off – though the tickets had already gone to the fans long before the EP (backed, in a manner which the band are still doing to this day, with tracks from older albums) blazed a trail up the charts. The album had a plain front with simple outline shots of the band's faces – a design suggested by Coverdale after their manager had presented them with artwork featuring yet another unclad female posterior. This time he got to put it where it belonged. "The band went crazy when they saw it. I'm just not interested in that sort of thing or you'd be right to accuse me of blatant sexism," Coverdale told a reporter during the tour.

The improvement of 'Lovehunter' over 'Trouble' had been clearly audible and the first few bars of 'Ready An' Willing' evinced another leap-forward in the overall sound, due this time to Ian Paice's drumming. Whereas before the drums had been fairly lightweight much of the time, here they pushed out of the mix, driving the band along. Indeed the opening 'Fool For Your Loving' existed almost solely on the bass and drums for much of the time. Even something as musically basic as 'Sweet Talker' came across as powerful and exciting.

In retrospect, this was the album they should have done at the start and it wasn't so much a progression from 'Trouble' and 'Lovehunter' as a consolidation of

the work begun there. In his new-found enthusiasm Coverdale went back to rework 'Blindman' and imbued it with a new sense of strength, though something of the melancholy and emotion which made the original so attractive was sacrificed for a heavier take. Coverdale has since gone back at regular intervals to reinterpret earlier Whitesnake material.

In the field within which Whitesnake had set out to work, they were rapidly reaching a peak. Reviewers were equally unanimous in their praise, some comparing the marriage of rock and blues to the classic Chicago blues and Styx sound of the sixties. Some may complain that the records don't sound 'modern': in a sense they never were, rather a reflection of the members' musical influences and loves, with nobody worrying particularly about how fashionable it all was.

Jon Lord backstage, 1980.

The proportion of fillers to decent tracks was also improving: by my reckoning only three of the tracks here call for the needle to be lifted. The band's reputation was even spreading across the Eastern Bloc, with Hungarian Radio providing local fans unable to secure the vinyl with a special broadcast of the album in Budapest, while 'Fool For Your Loving' made a rare official vinyl appearance as a single in Poland.

Just before they hit the road in Britain Coverdale, Murray and Paice did a few local radio shows to help promote the tour and up at Radio Clyde Paice got to do his DJ for the night bit, complaining about Hendrix's 'Stone Free', "I still can't do the drum pattern, I've tried for years now. Either Mitchell dubbed the cowbell on or he's a lot better than I think he is," he told listeners.

Supported by Gary Moore's G-Force, the tour went well and in an effort to sort out problems generated by the Japanese live set, the band used The Rolling Stones' Mobile to tape the climax of the tour – two sold out shows at London's Hammersmith Odeon. With the album selling well (it went into the charts at number nine) and the EP in the Top 20, it was fairly clear that the band had really broken in Britain, while the audience reaction at many shows was amazing.

Steering clear of heavy metal as they'd done, Whitesnake were able to reach out and touch the crowds in a way that most metal music could never hope to. "That's the whole point of Whitesnake, we share. When you smash down that barrier between audience and group it's an unbelievable, indescribable feeling." It was happening more and more often now the band had found a line-up which sparked. Some of the later dates had to be juggled around a little to allow David time to get over a bout of laryngitis diagnosed

Whitesnake festival appearances, 1980.

Ian Paice at Sheffield, June 1980.

during the tour. A useful precaution, so he was in good form for the London shows. The cancelled gigs were slotted in a week later.

The tour was done on a fairly strict security basis, a departure from earlier years, and the band were whisked away promptly after each gig. In his defence (as journalists seized on the fact with glee) Coverdale pointed out that most of the fans had got their autographs on the previous tour and this time they wanted to get away in a reasonable time since Lord and Paice both drove home after many of the shows. "You want my job?" Coverdale offered one journalist who bravely pressed him on the apparent about turn. "There's no change in this band's attitude to the kids, there's no change in our motivation to give and to fucking share but if I stay for three hours at the gig tonight and then three hours the next night I'll be too knackered to do a proper show."

He also rightly pointed out that previously the band had been touring during the winter months and having people back for autographs at least stopped them freezing to death at the stage door, whereas this year they were actually ahead of schedule, trying to make time for more forays to foreign parts once the UK dates were out of the way. Perhaps he was just anxious to get back to the hotel for the Moody and Marsden show,

the pair having hired pantomime horses to liven up residents and to try and phase hotel porters.

Accompanied by head roadie Magnet, who earned his nickname back in Purple days for his never failing ability to secure females for after hours entertainment with the group, they performed a Fred Astaire number in the foyer to attract one receptionist's attention. After the time-honoured, "Can I help you sir?" Magnet was able to keep a straight face and reply, "No thanks, I'm with the horse."

Lack of rehearsal time restricted the quantity of new material. 'Blindman' was intended as a replacement for the ageing 'Mistreated', but despite an airing at Liverpool wasn't added to the show anywhere else, while talk of adding 'Only My Soul' to the set sadly turned out to be just talk. The set reached back only as far as 'Snakebite', kicking off with 'Come On' and 'Sweet Talker'. 'Walking In The Shadow Of The Blues' put the studio version firmly in its place and became one of the most powerful tracks of the show, as well as a firm indication of the style the band had adopted.

'Ain't Gonna Cry No More' also benefited from the energy of a live performance, a long sweeping blues-based track driven by the power of Murray and Paice. Opening gently with Marsden on 12-string and Lord's atmospheric keyboard work, the song suddenly opened up with the band hammering in, glorious stuff. 'Lovehunter' was followed by 'Mistreated', the only oldie left in the show. Coverdale delivered some frightening performances of the number during the tour, with an intensity and delivery I've never heard anyone equal.

To give him a chance to relax a little they stuck in 'Nighthawk' (a track christened by David's mother, it was her nickname for him) and 'Belgian Tom's Hat-Trick', the instrumental romp which allowed the guitars some fun while Coverdale psyched himself up for 'Ain't No Love In The Heart Of The City'. Hit single time in the form of 'Fool For Your Loving' took the concert towards a climax, the shows ending with a massive version of 'Take Me With You'. If the band were asked back for more (and so far as I know they always were) 'Ready An' Willing' and 'Lie Down' provided the encores. The excitement and promise of the previous year's tour had been more than justified and in general the shows scaled new heights.

Midway through the tour members of Bad Company turned up to help Jon Lord celebrate another year on the road, yet another excuse for snide comments in some of the papers, while the record company made a vague attempt to emulate the success of 'Fool For Your Loving' by issuing another three-track EP during the tour. By this time most people had got the album anyway and it failed to do business. They also issued the repackaged 'Trouble' album to cash in on the band's growing following. Whitesnake filled in time after the tour by starting work on the next album down at Startling Studios in Ascot, owned by Ringo Starr, as well as forming part of an *ad hoc* group to play at Bernie Marsden's wedding.

August was festival time again. At the first Donington bash Cozy Powell was playing his last show with Rainbow, while Whitesnake headlined down at Reading, a show taped (as the previous year) by the BBC for airing on radio. A strange set, Jon left out his musical references to Purple which had been part of his solos to date (and which no longer threatened to steal the show), while Paice didn't get a solo at all. Otherwise the show followed the same set as the UK tour.

All the Deep Purple reunion talk had prompted Neil, Bernie and Micky to have T-shirts printed up which from a distance looked like DP designs. Only on closer inspection did they reveal the legend, 'No I Wasn't In Deep Fucking Purple'. "The Purple thing never really worried us, the kids shout out for Whitesnake songs not old Purple numbers," Bernie Marsden explained after being asked how he felt about the situation. "I play golf with Cozy Powell and the first one to mention Deep Purple loses five strokes."

Ian Paice celebrated the birth of his first daughter when his horse, Miss Raffles, romped home in first place with Lester Piggott aboard. Ian had dabbled in horse racing since Purple days, more often than not ending up "with a donkey" so it was a relief to find a successful horse at last. At least it got the rest of the band off his back, since they continually blamed him for losing their money when his horses lost. There was little time to relax. Recording sessions continued after Reading, as well as overdubbing and mixing the Hammersmith tapes into a presentable album.

Leaving Martin Birch to finish the live album,

Marsden & Moody provide karaoke backing for actor John Hurt, Munich, November 1980.

Startling Studios, where Come And Get It was laid down, July 1980.

Martin Birch, Deep Purple's producer who went on to produce Whitesnake's first few albums.

Whitesnake departed in early October for their first real tour of America. They were asked by Jethro Tull to do the tour as their guests, so the visit wasn't as financially crippling as it could have been, although with 12 crew, two coaches, the gear truck and hotel bills, they still had little change out of £200,000. The band had to prune their set, taking it down to the regulation 45 minutes. Rather than do a short set then waste time coming back to encore they took the decision to make the maximum use of their allotted time. Coverdale explained the reasons: "We started rehearsing and we timed the show and said, 'Well we'll cut this out, cut out the drum solo, shorten this bit' and it was still like an hour. With 'Ready An' Willing' the only really known album we said we'd concentrate mostly on that. It's difficult to make that transition from headliner to opener but it's also very necessary. There's no way we could afford as Whitesnake to take our production to America."

Coverdale realised the billing was less than he'd expected. "My memory of Tull was in the halcyon days of rock and it is not really a rock audience they attract." It took a while to get into their new role but before long they were making an impression. "What the hell's goin' on?" one journalist demanded to know. "This ain't no opening act." The audience restraint was something else the band had to get used to, no standing at the back and no dancing in the aisles or else; a far cry from the sweaty crush at the St Georges Hall in Bradford or the Sporthalle in Köln. At least the early finish gave them time to party after the show. Relaxing in one hotel, the singer with the house band suddenly recognised Coverdale in the room; launching into 'Smoke On The Water' (at one time Americans' most popular tune after their national anthem) she invited Coverdale to help. Once up and running, he couldn't be stopped. Marsden and Murray were not long in joining him and soon they were racing through 'Jailhouse Rock', 'Blue Suede Shoes' *et al.* The singer must have wished she'd never seen him before. Mirage made an effort with several tracks issued as singles but otherwise seemed at a loss as to how to tackle the band.

Whitesnake went down reasonably well in some

areas, mostly in the South and West but elsewhere it was hard going. Touring resulted in a fair amount of airplay for 'Fool For Your Loving' and the album crept up to the middle sixties in the Billboard charts. As Coverdale put it, seeds had been sown. The tour ended after a month, the band swinging on into Germany as special guests on the November/December AC/DC tour. AC/DC being yer straight forward metallers, it seemed a less than appropriate billing and indeed they managed to attract airborne missiles in Paris, but things generally went well with AC/DC being responsive to the needs of their support band. "Their attitude," reported Coverdale, "is do whatever you want." As Whitesnake had already headlined, some fans were disgruntled at having to pay full whack for a shortened support slot but understanding roadies at some gigs were ready with a refund on the ticket price.

The strain of a year on the road was also beginning to tell though, as Coverdale explained to a reporter out to cover the dates. "This is one of the lowest ebbs we have ever been at, physically and mentally very very tired. If we can get through this tour and then go to hospital for Christmas . . ." Many a true word. They managed to get on to German TV miming to a couple of tracks and when Jon Lord failed to materialise had to do it as a five-piece. For a laugh Bernie Marsden suggested that he and Neil Murray swop instruments for one number – only to have the smile wiped off his face when Murray slipped in the dry ice at the end and trashed one of Marsden's prized guitars.

During the show at Saarbrucken, Coverdale too managed to overdo the footwork and torn ligaments in his right leg forced the cancellation of the final few dates. "As I jumped up and did a body swerve I landed awkwardly, but I carried on, doing an encore supported by my mike stand. I was in a cast for three months, in fact I did 'Come An' Get It' on crutches. It could have been worse, as we were in Hamburg at the time I went to see the local football team specialist who fixed me up, otherwise it might have been permanently damaged." One way to get home early for Christmas but painful nevertheless.

Cheerier news was waiting back home . . . the album had gone gold. For Whitesnake fans the year ended at last to pick up the Hammersmith recordings when 'Live . . . In The Heart Of The City' was made available. This consisted of the recording from earlier in the year and, as a bonus, the 1978 recording issued in Japan was given away with it. A drag for those who had coughed up for the import perhaps, for whom a more complete version of the 1980 tape might have been more acceptable, yet a nice gesture for fans as the double set only cost a quid more than a normal single album (the band taking a cut in royalties to enable this). UA decided they couldn't run to a gatefold cover, though several other countries were less stingy.

There had been plans to tour America at the end of the year as a support to Molly Hatchet but this was abandoned even before Coverdale's accident, although manager John Coletta was quite keen on it for a time. "I haven't heard this Molly Hatchet but I believe she's very big in America." "How is your relationship with your manager?" quizzed one reporter that same month. "Pass."

VII

1981
'COME AN' GET IT'
ALBUM AND TOUR

Previous Page: Donington 1981.

As they'd done the previous year, Whitesnake kicked 1981 off in the studio, this time back in Startling for the third and last stint on the next album. There was also time for some of the band to indulge in extra-curricular activities. Micky Moody found himself a little earner penning the tune for the new Levi's TV commercial, with vocals by Rainbow front man Graham Bonnet, who would also use Moody on his upcoming solo album, along with another Rainbow refugee Cozy Powell and Whitesnakers Neil Murray and Jon Lord. If that wasn't enough he was still working off and on with Bob Young and in his spare time became involved with Lemmy's favourite band, The Nolans.

Following the album's completion, Whitesnake busied themselves with photo sessions, video shoots and reshoots, a couple of TV slots and rehearsals at Bray studios to work on a new stage set. In between all this Bernie Marsden rattled off his second solo album with help from some of the band, and about the same time his first finally found a British release (mysteriously losing the Bobby Dazzler alias in the process).

Musically it was quite a contrast to Whitesnake, much more American in style, though it did have guest places for Paice, Lord and Murray as well as Cozy Powell, Don Airey and assorted mates. Whitesnake's own album 'Come An' Get It' was on time for April release and the recommencement of touring, kicking off with a fortnight on the road in Germany. This time they were headlining with a vengeance, assisted by the rabble rousing Slade and making up for shows cancelled at the back end of 1980. They managed to fit in a couple of shows in Scandinavia too, though trouble loomed when they turned up in Copenhagen to find the concert stage in a dangerous state, unable to support the weight of their gear, resulting in a cancellation. Apart from that and Micky Moody collapsing in Hamburg after overheating underneath one of those wide brimmed hats he insisted on wearing, the band were in good form by the time the British tour came around.

Once again the album provided another killer punch, this time with a fine romp called 'Don't Break My Heart Again', even if Neil Murray would have been happy never to hear it again. "David kept me awake all night because he was trying out this riff on the organ, which was right under my bedroom in the studio." It was worth a sleepless night, emulating their chart success of the previous year and helping the album to the top of the UK hit parade. Despite the good sales (it entered the charts at number two and sold 100,000 copies) the album was generally a disappointment after the energy of its predecessor.

Somehow that vital spark was missing for much of the time and despite some professional performances only a few tracks came up to scratch; 'Hit And Run' and 'Girl' showed promise though the former caused problems in the studio when Ian Paice dried up and was unable to provide an intro for the track. "We ended up cracking up," recalled Coverdale of the moment. "He couldn't feel an intro. I was saying to Paicey 'Just think of Dag, Dag, Dagenham' which if you listen to it . . . fabulous intro." 'Til The Day I Die' – even if it was 'Ain't Gonna Cry No More' revisited – closed the second side in fine style.

Elsewhere the sparser instrumentation threw much more attention on the vocals and Coverdale sounded

Top & Middle: Jon Lord & Micky Moody begin work on Saints and Sinners, November 1981.

unconvincing at times. ''I don't think there's anything new, I think it's just an extension of the band being stronger as a unit. It's good but I don't think we're going to challenge any contemporary art fashions,'' Coverdale mused soon after the release.

If things were thus a little shaky in the studio, there was little evidence of it on-stage. For the first time the band headlined some of the larger British venues, places like the Leisure Centre at Deeside and the Granby Halls in Leicester. Like many others I prefer my gigs in smaller places, where you can feel a part of the action, without necessarily getting crushed to death against scaffolding at the head of 10,000 people all craning for a glimpse of the stage. Yet Whitesnake were now reaching the stage where ticket demand outstripped available seats, short of the band spending the rest of their days on the road here.

In an effort to balance the situation they also included some of the more traditional gigs, doubling up at Newcastle City Hall for example to try to satisfy demand. The problem was what to do in London? In the end they fought shy of Wembley and instead sold out five shows at Hammersmith Odeon, four in a row followed by a fifth night a week later (with proceeds from one show going to charity). Attempts were made to film one performance for a video but the cameras got in the way and a power failure in the set put paid to that, although Coverdale's, ''Get these fucking cameras out of the way,'' might have made life difficult in the editing room.

Billy Squier, the support, made an attempt to poach Jon Lord during the tour. Responding to criticism from certain quarters, both he and Paice curtailed their solos, instead working out in fine style along with Neil Murray during 'Belgian Tom's Hat-Trick', an oldie which earned its curious title back in 1978 during Whitesnake's club tour. Chatting with a girl after a show in Scarborough, Moody confessed that like her he had gypsy origins, coming as he did from Belgium. ''She said I sounded like a northerner, so I said 'Yes, North Belgium'. I'd also told her my name was Tom for some reason.''

A long night ensued and Coverdale christened the event Belgian Tom's Hat-Trick. 'Come An' Get It' wasn't plundered too heavily for material though naturally 'Don't Break My Heart Again' was included, while 'Wine, Women An' Song' provided a suitable bit of nonsense to close the shows. Whitesnake played to some 130,000 people on the UK tour.

Proof that the so called heavy metal revival was well under way came with the first issue of Britain's first magazine devoted to the genre, *Kerrang!*, with Coverdale making the cover of issue three. With this kind of success, talk of a Deep Purple reunion began to fade at last, but according to their former manager four million had been offered to the three relevant Whitesnake members if they would join forces with Roger Glover and Ritchie Blackmore for three months' work as Deep Purple. A second Japanese tour was arranged for June; here too the band were beginning to break.

Then there was the festival at Donington. True to form it rained, but Whitesnake managed to pull off a good show despite the circumstances, Jon Lord stealing it for most people, though the band felt that the break in touring caused by the American cancellations had left them a little rusty. As an experiment, the keyboards were set up on a riser next to the drum kit, so for once Jon Lord wasn't half hidden by the PA, while the others had more room at the front. The idea wasn't retained, for after 15 years or so stage left Lord found it hard to cope with being moved.

More seriously, Neil Murray, sandwiched between the two, found it hard to hear what was going on, while Coverdale suffered through the bass amps coming straight at him. Musically the set was more or less the same as the previous tour, with a verse or two of the old Spencer Davis hit 'Gimme Some Loving' slipped in during the encore. Many thought Whitesnake deserved top billing and realised that they'd actually played for longer than bill toppers AC/DC.

While they had the gear out of storage, the group responded to the pleas of fans from Scotland where the shows earlier in the year had been difficult for many to get to. Two concerts at the Edinburgh Playhouse were slotted in a week after Donington. Jon Lord's old mate Tony Ashton sat in the wings with comedian Billy Connolly getting some serious head shaking done.

The trip to Scotland came in handy for Micky Moody and Neil Murray who were able to sneak off and find Edinburgh's Army And Navy Stores. They'd seen donkey jackets on offer in *Exchange And Mart* at a price that was too good to miss. Meanwhile Bernie Marsden's second solo set hit the stores in August. He did a special Radio One session to promote it with Coverdale helping out on vocals, Murray, Philips and Airey forming the band for the show.

After five months on the road, there was a month off before work began on the next album. Jon Lord took the opportunity to begin his own album in Britannia Studios. Until now all Jon's solo work had tended to evolve from his love of classical music, which began in earnest back in 1969 when Deep Purple played alongside The Royal Philharmonic Orchestra. The 'Gemini Suite' followed and then the partially successful 'Windows' (on which David Coverdale had also sung). This side of Lord's career culminated in the extraordinarily beautiful 'Sarabande' album issued in late 1976. Since then he had toyed with the idea of another album along the same lines but in the end decided to go for a more conventional set of tracks utilising musicians from the Whitesnake circle.

Most of the material was written by the time he reached the studio, so it was done with a minimum of fuss. Neil Murray, Ian Paice and David Coverdale all helped out – though in the end Coverdale's contributions were left in the can – while other names were familiar from earlier projects: Kirke, Ralphs, Philips, Powell and Tony Ashton. As soon as the initial sessions had been taped, Whitesnake assembled to begin work for their new album. Lord had been using Guy Bidmead to produce his material so when the band decided to find someone other than Martin Birch, he was the obvious choice. After a few days rehearsing the band began recording down at Shepperton, partly because it was handy for Lord and Paice but they quickly decided the sound wasn't what they were after so most of the backing tracks were redone over the next four weeks at Clearwell, using a mobile recording studio.

Donington 1981.

As the work continued it became clear that the album/tour/album routine was beginning to tell. While the band as a whole were a little weary, Micky Moody in particular was becoming disillusioned. "Even at the beginning of 1981, that European tour that we did, it was partly my fault. I'd been enjoying myself too much, drinking too much and it began to get to me a little bit, plus the novelty was wearing off. I think we realised by then we weren't going to crack the States, that ill fated Judas Priest tour. I felt we weren't going to go anywhere."

Recording sessions were interrupted by three weeks of dates, mainly in Germany but opening in Paris, supported once more by Billy Squier who although fairly unknown here had sold over two million albums back home in America. The visit was quickly dubbed the Black Ice Tour, partly because of another in-band joke which led to Neil Murray being dubbed Captain Black Ice in best Mutiny On The Bounty tones, but also because bad weather caused problems throughout and prevented many fans from even getting to the shows. To cap it all Ian Paice was diagnosed as having contracted mumps from his son – bad enough in children but a serious disease in adults. They were forced to pull out; another German tour had bitten the dust.

CHAPTER VIII

1982

'SAINTS AN' SINNERS', POWELL, GALLEY, HODGKINSON JOINING

During January the band were in and out of Britannia Row adding to the already completed material. Micky Moody went along one night to complete some guitar parts. "I was pissed off, there was just me there and it was time for a solo on one track which was 'Victim Of Love', well I ended up just taking the piss, doing car horn noises and things. I had a few personal things which were affecting me too."

Clearly the situation was deteriorating and towards the end of the recordings Coverdale called a band meeting, and announced that he was putting Whitesnake on hold for the time being. Over the Christmas break Coverdale had taken stock of the situation and decided the time had come to sort out the future of Whitesnake before things got any worse.

During the last German tour he'd felt things were not going as well as they ought. Coverdale had been pissed off on one occasion when he turned round during his 'Soldier Of Fortune' solo and found Moody and Marsden enjoying a joke together, but it was only when he returned to complete the new album that it all came to a head. He'd written several new numbers, yet he felt that the others were too wrapped up in solo projects of one sort or another and weren't giving 100 per cent to the band.

"I took over the completion of the album and said to the others, 'I make no promises to any of you. If you get an opportunity to join someone, please take it.' The band just seemed happy cruising with all that success and they lost their hunger. When we came to record our album I couldn't handle the apathy." Marsden and Moody's contribution to the band had, apart from the musical side, always been as the jokers – with endless gags to while away the boredom of life on the road. Coverdale hadn't minded too much but felt that during the recordings this side of things had got in the way of the music.

Even Ian Paice came in for some stick. For some time he'd been experimenting with a less flashy style of playing, simpler and more economical, influenced perhaps by American drummers as well as the very direct approach of John Bonham. To an extent unsure of this new style, he became very worried about his playing and it was showing in his performance. In a sense things had become too cosy, too matey, with little of the edge that usually provides the spark a band needs. Nevertheless it was something that Coverdale should have perhaps nipped in the bud earlier.

As well as his unhappiness with the attitudes in the band, Coverdale was even less pleased with his management and decided to make a clean break there too. Not surprisingly this was by no means straightforward and Coverdale realised it would take some time to do. Putting the band on hold seemed the best option. Micky Moody decided to call it a day. "I didn't know what was going on and I didn't really care. I spoke to David and he said, 'I'm putting the band on ice' or on a holding pattern or whatever and I said fair enough, I've had enough anyway." For a while Coverdale was uncertain whether to replace him or leave things as they were. Obviously it was a blow, Moody having written much of the band's material.

Time passed, the upcoming March UK tour which had originally been set to coincide with the new album was shelved. Taking advantage of the lull, Jon Lord

completed his solo album and toured as part of the Olympic Rock And Blues Circus, a project that evolved from work done by rock drummers Pete York and Charlie Eichert for an LP the previous year. They decided to perform some live shows and when the keyboard player who had done the album was unavailable, Pete York contacted Lord. Vocalist was Chris Farlowe and on bass Colin Hodgkinson helped out.

The brief tour ended in early April, after which Whitesnake planned to visit Japan. This was ditched and at another meeting Bernie Marsden was fired. Marsden had already written material for a third solo album and hoped to play some live gigs to support it. He began auditioning for new band members almost at once and by August his new group S.O.S. were up and gigging, with Richard Bailey on keyboards. At that same meeting, Coletta announced he had come to an arrangement to relinquish control of the band, though Bernie Marsden remained one of his acts.

Whitesnake were now guitarless. With Coverdale keeping a strict silence during this period, rumours began to fly. There was talk of him auditioning for the Michael Schenker Group, even to replace Paul Rodgers in Bad Company. As far as MSG were concerned, Coverdale was under consideration for a time and had been approached to work on the 'Nuclear Assault' album but turned it down. "He (Cozy) approached me in January this year and asked me to join the Marks And Spencer Group, we sat up all night talking but I decided against joining. Then I had the idea of incorporating them into Whitesnake. I spent a long time thinking what to do."

If the idea of teaming up with MSG was out (especially when he discovered they were to be managed by John Coletta), he was interested in their drummer, Cozy Powell. The pair had met on several occasions in the past and talked of working together when Cozy was offered a job in the band back in 1979. On the guitar front various names were also being bandied about . . . Mick Ralphs, Pink Floyd's Dave Gilmour and even Jimmy Page. This latter story was lapped up in the American press once the ever reliable *Daily Mirror* came up with the 'exclusive', while Boz Burrell was tipped for the post of bassist. "I haven't seen Jimmy in about six years," David later explained in

May 8, 1982

sden's exit signals
for Whitesnake

WHITESNAKE are now axe-less following the departure of Bernie Marsden (pictured left) last week to pursue a solo career. Earlier this year fellow guitarist Micky Moody left the band, who've reportedly been having problems recording a new album. Indeed, there's no word on when a new Whitesnake album is expected and Marsden's departure can only increase speculation over the group's future.

Bernie Marsden said last week: "The split was totally amicable. I just felt the need for a change. I'm sure I'll be working with David Coverdale in a writing capacity in the future and I wish him the best of luck."

Marsden is now putting together his own band and plans to go out on tour after the World Cup is over. He'll be recording his third solo album during the summer and intends playing British dates to coincide with its release. These dates are likely to include a couple of festival appearances.

Whitesnake keyboard player Jon Lord has also been recording a solo album during the band's hiatus and it will be released by EMI at the end of June under the title 'Before I Forget'. A single called 'Bach Onto This' will be released on May 25.

Left: Lord relaxing during the Olympic Rock & Blues Circus tour, Germany, March 1982.
Above: Marsden, UK tour, 1981.
Right: Guy Bidmead, briefly produced Whitesnake, January 1982.

order to set the record straight. "Also I'm not really into the guitar hero system." In fact he had already approached Mel Galley about the job.

Mel Galley was born in Cannock, Staffordshire, on March 8, 1948 and his first musical experience was helping his elder brother write songs. Learning the guitar, the pair formed a group called The Interns, who evolved into first The News and then Finders Keepers who recorded a handful of singles in the late sixties. They were joined on one by Glenn Hughes, another local lad, and in 1968 he and Mel Galley and others went on to form Trapeze. Signed up by local stars The Moody Blues, who had formed their own record label, Trapeze's début album issued in 1970 was perhaps influenced rather too much by their peers. However, the five-piece didn't last long and a split within the band saw Galley, Hughes and drummer Dave Holland continuing on the Trapeze name. They soon developed into a much harder outfit — one reviewer even compared their second-album to Led Zeppelin's early output.

Trapeze's hard funky rock style found favour in

Britain on a small scale but in America their southern boogie influences earned them a much larger following, and it was their constant US touring, where they were managed by the same promoter who handled ZZ Top, which kept them afloat over the next few years. The constant touring was very wearing however and in 1973 the band decided to expand to a four-piece. Fate decreed otherwise; one of Trapeze's shows had been seen by members of Deep Purple who, impressed with Hughes' bass playing and singing, made him an offer he found hard to refuse. Trapeze soldiered on through several line-up changes with Mel Galley determined to see them on to better days, even to the extent of turning down offers from David Coverdale in 1977.

The band finally bowed out in 1981 and Galley turned his hand to sessions and even returned to his original trade as a carpenter from time to time. Ironically it was his carpentry which brought him into Whitesnake. Maurice Jones, one of the organisers of the Donington Festival, asked Mel if he was interested in lending his woodworking skills for the 1981 show and it was there that he bumped into David Coverdale in the backstage area. Coverdale explained that all was not what it should be within the band and that if he got a new line-up together would Mel be interested? The answer was yes.

In June Jon Lord's album 'Before I Forget' reached the stores but the end results sounded more like Lord and his friends enjoying themselves in the studio than attempting anything overly creative. Covering everything from fifteenth century tunes through rocked up Bach compositions to rhythm and blues, it suffered from a lack of unity and although he was able to take advantage of the Whitesnake hiatus to embark on a thorough round of promotional interviews, the album didn't stay on catalogue for very long.

Neil Murray didn't wait around to see what might or might not happen. He busied himself with a session for Gary Moore (they'd been in Collosseum II together), some rehearsals with Jeff Beck and a couple of live gigs and some demos with a band called Badlands, along with guitarist John Sykes. That didn't arouse much interest so Sykes went off to join Thin Lizzy and Neil Murray joined Ian Paice to help Gary Moore record his new album, 'Corridors Of Power'. For a time Gary Moore was looking a possible candidate for Whitesnake,

Modelling their leathers, 1982.

though he didn't really fancy having to take second place in a band again and certainly didn't relish the idea of the dual guitar line-up which was one of Whitesnake's trademarks. As Coverdale had already approached Mel Galley once more to play lead, this was awkward, though he did consider asking Galley to switch to bass to accommodate Moore. In the end Gary Moore decided to continue with his own career.

On August 5 Coverdale was finally free of his old management contract. To celebrate he departed for a camping holiday on Dartmoor with Cozy Powell and ex-SAS man John Ferguson, sometime bodyguard to the stars but now employed preparing the groundwork for the band's next tour. "I wanted to get myself fit again so we went on a sort of commando course," Cozy told one journalist. "It did us a lot of good. I did most of

the cooking, I had to do everything actually, David is not the most outdoor person I've ever met. David's contribution consisted mainly of trying to buy a cup of tea in one of the small villages using his American Express card.''

Back in civilisation the two were approached by Tony Iommi who was interested in filling the depleted Black Sabbath ranks. Coverdale, refreshed by his hiking holiday, was by now determined to reforge Whitesnake, though his idea of sending all prospective members on a week's survival course on Dartmoor armed only with a penknife and a six pack of baked beans probably didn't find much enthusiasm. John Coletta meantime, despite having lost David Coverdale, still had his eye open for a potential money earner. Casting his eye over to Eastern Europe and the rock starved fans behind the Iron

Curtain, he approached the remnants of Whitesnake and asked them if they'd be interested in doing a few festivals over there under the name of Deep Purple. "We said forget it," Neil Murray laughed as he recalled Coletta's approach.

In mid-August Coverdale called yet another meeting to set out the current situation. Powell and Galley were joining Whitesnake and Jon Lord would be staying on. "Lordy enhances my songs more than any other musician I've worked with," Coverdale explained later. He'd not chosen a second guitarist though Billy Rankin was under consideration, while he wasn't sure if Neil Murray's style of bass playing would work with Cozy Powell's forthright drumming (even though the pair had worked together in the past).

Cozy (Colin) Powell was born on December 29, 1947 in Cirencester, Gloucestershire. His first band was The Sorcerers whom he joined in 1965 after leaving school. With them Powell (who was nicknamed after the famous drummer Cozy Cole) spent many months touring German night clubs, often doing several shows a night. It was this (and weight training in later years) which he reckons helped build up his incredible stamina. Powell stuck it for several years barring a brief spell with Casey Jones And The Engineers. The Sorcerers evolved into The Ace Kefford Stand and he began to spend his spare time doing session work for pop supremo Mickie Most.

Powell then teamed up with Dave Clempson to record a single and do a few shows under the name of Big Bertha but Jeff Beck, who was also involved with Most doing some tacky singles, saw Powell in the studio in 1970 and asked him to audition. Powell did two albums with him, leaving in July 1972 when Beck went off to start BB&A. He formed Bedlam (originally named Beast) towards the end of that year and they stuck it out for one album. However, finances were not all they might have been and Powell continued to do sessions on the side to earn a living, drifting into a downward spiral of turning out drum instrumentals for Mickie Most along with a bunch of Most's session men. Worse still, some of them were massive UK hits – 'Dance With The Devil' and 'The Man In Black' saw him appearing regularly on *Top Of The Pops*. Yet away from the charts, Powell was forging a heavy band – and the teeny boppers turning up at the local Locarno were doubtless somewhat confused when confronted with the outcome.

In May 1974 he formed Cozy Powell's Hammer with Bernie Marsden on guitar and (briefly) Neil Murray on bass. It was fun for a time but soon became hard going and after a year he jacked it in. Three months later former Deep Purple guitarist Ritchie Blackmore was casting about for a new drummer as he set about remodelling his new group Rainbow. Remembering Powell from his days with Beck, Blackmore gave him a call. Powell, after a very brief stint with Strange Brew (who posed for pictures but split before even rehearsing), had turned his back on music and returned to his other passion, motor racing, when Ritchie called in early September 1975. Rainbow's line-up changes were legendary in rock circles, as much for the manner in which they occurred as anything else. Powell stuck it longer than most – longer than anyone except Blackmore himself.

This was probably because he was one of the few musicians able to keep up with Blackmore; nor would he take too much crap, giving as good as he got. The early Rainbow days were fruitful musically, but expensive, and Blackmore soon found himself in a financially difficult situation. Rather than knock the band on the head, he went for the other option and commercialised the music. Casting round for help he took on board one of the old Deep Purple writing team, Roger Glover, who did what was required, and the revamped Rainbow soon found themselves regular performers (albeit via video) on *Top Of The Pops*.

This wasn't achieved without alienating many of the band's earlier admirers, one of whom was Cozy Powell. After refusing to do more than one take of the horrendous 'Since You Been Gone', he decided that if this was the course Blackmore was setting for Rainbow, then he wanted out. Blackmore didn't heed the warnings and after headlining the UK Donington Monsters Of Rock festival in August 1980 Powell bowed out to team up with the Michael Schenker Group to be joined there briefly by ex-Rainbow vocalist Graham Bonnet in February of 1982.

"It started off good," Cozy commented on his stint with MSG, "then dwindled away. The amount of rehearsing finally did me in. We spent three months rehearsing, every day. You don't rehearse heavy metal." In the end Powell gave Michael Schenker an ultimatum: "Either we get on and go into the studio and record, or count me out. So he counted me out." Coverdale was on the phone within days and Powell accepted the offer of a seat in Whitesnake. Powell himself came in for a bit of stick for what some journalists saw as a never ending round of chopping and changing, though in truth his career had been far less erratic than people made out. "Look at Aynsley Dunbar," Cozy pointed out in his defence. "He's been in eight bands in five years." Ian Paice's services were obviously no longer needed and he accepted Gary Moore's offer of a permanent place in his band.

With no firm word from Coverdale, Neil Murray also joined for a couple of low-key Marquee gigs prior to a spot on the bill at Reading. As Whitesnake's wages had stopped some time back he had to pay the rent somehow. It wasn't until the end of September that he was offered his job back in Whitesnake but by then he had decided instead to give Gary Moore a try. In between trying to rebuild Whitesnake, Coverdale returned to the studios to lay down vocals on the album and the following month phoned up Micky Moody to offer him his job back. Moody had been down to Reading to jam on one number with Marsden's new band SOS. After the show Marsden persuaded Moody to tag along for another show at a secret venue. It wasn't until the pair of them entered Marsden's house to the strains of 'Happy Birthday' that Moody twigged. "He'd organised a surprise party. Everybody was there, it was like *This Is Your Life*. Then David was on the phone to wish me Happy Birthday, asking me how it was going and he said he was getting the band together with Mel and would I like to come back in."

"Micky regained the root feeling I thought he'd lost at the end of 81," Coverdale explained. Five months had given him time to rest and sort himself out, although going without wages for so long was probably

Jon Lord's old Hammond groans under the weight of additional keyboards, Leeds Queen's Hall, May 1981.

a contributory factor. Along with Mel Galley, he was rushed into the studios to do backing vocals and put down a proper solo on 'Victim Of Love'. At the same time Martin Birch was asked to remix the tapes. The group were restored to full strength by the arrival of Colin Hodgkinson, primarily at the suggestion of Lord who had worked with him earlier in the year.

Colin Hodgkinson was born in Peterborough on October 14, 1945 and had joined Backdoor, a highly respected jazz-rock trio from the north east of England, in 1971. He stayed with them for nearly six years, then worked with Journey's Neal Schon and did two albums with Jan Hammer. He also played bass on Cozy Powell's upcoming solo album 'Octopuss', recorded at Britannia Row during September and October 1982, so he was known to them all. Coverdale in particular was a big fan of Backdoor and Hodgkinson's bass style. By October they were able to announce plans for a full British tour, to stretch through from the end of 1982 into the New Year. Finally EMI began the vinyl assault with 'Here I Go Again', issued as a taster on October 30 – a fairly apt summing up of the band's state of affairs title wise.

In America, where Whitesnake enjoyed a brief spell on Liberty again after EMI bought the label out, Coverdale signed a new deal with Geffen Records to include Canada and Japan. Their A&R man John Kalodner, an almost legendary talent spotter, saw Coverdale on stage and felt certain he could bring the band that long-sought American success.

Titled 'Saints And Sinners' (even though Steve Gibbons and Johnny Winter had both done LPs of that name), the new album reached the stores on November 15 having been in production for over a year. In view of the already overlong delay Coverdale decided to issue it more or less as it was; indeed he had little option due to contractual obligations. As if to emphasise the nature of the problems, credits were left off the LP altogether and the back cover featured just a single live photo of Coverdale, while the front featured a kitschy sculpture of the kind some folk insist on decorating their mantelpieces with.

Today the album remains one of their weakest, although it does hint at the transition from the traditional Whitesnake style toward the harder musical approach which was slowly emerging, especially on tracks like 'Victim Of Love'. Overall the sound is poor and not particularly well mixed, with the keyboards lost and the bass relegated to some far distant place.

At times the material manages to overcome such problems, especially the excellent 'Crying In The Rain' which builds some promise, but elsewhere the limits of the band's writing as well as the upheavals during the recording were apparent. It wasn't even issued in America. Honest as ever, Jon Lord agreed with some of the criticism. "It's not my job to sit here and make excuses, but . . . the backing tracks were made under quite difficult circumstances in terms of the band itself and the producer. His bottle really went when confronted with what we wanted, plus we went through about 19 different studios. It had to be released though, otherwise we would have been sued from here to Christmas.

"I became disillusioned from time to time, it was

a difficult time because I don't feel Ian Paice was very happy in the band – I know for a fact that he's much happier with Gary Moore – but overall there seemed to be a mood of unsureness and I know it affected the album. Sales did show that it wasn't as well received as it could have been. It sounds a bit 'down' though if you put it against 'Ready An' Willing' which I think is the best studio album . . .''

Well, it depends on which sales figures you look at because the album had gone gold by the end of the year, helped by the success of the single 'Here I Go Again' which became a hit right across Europe – even if it didn't climb quite as high in the UK charts as some of the band's earlier singles. ''Sinners was a struggle from start to finish,'' Coverdale wearily explained.

Whitesnake were back in action at Southampton's Gaumont early in December after 18 months off the road in Britain and the Saints And Sinners World Tour was underway, ticket sales unharmed by the long lay off. Overall the new line-up looked a little shaky as they hit the road for the first time in 12 months and had they not been under such pressure, longer rehearsals might have tightened things up. Coverdale himself showed few signs of having been away for so long. If Micky Moody had regained his lost enthusiasm however, his performance on-stage didn't always show it, his solo spot tending to duplicate that of previous tours. Colin Hodgkinson failed to stamp his character on the band as far as most people were concerned, though technically his solo spot turned a few heads. The shows were certainly heavier than anything Whitesnake had previously delivered but some of the subtlety had been forsaken in the process.

'Mistreated' was laid to rest in favour of 'Crying In The Rain' from the new LP, which formed the core of the set. Coverdale pushed the performance to its limits, putting the studio version to shame, with Mel Galley contributing some beefy but atmospheric guitar work. The track wound down with the immortal 'Soldier Of Fortune' verse to rapt attention from the crowds.

Drained, Coverdale as usual took off to grab a breather and left it to the soloists, with Jon Lord doing a turn followed by Cozy Powell . . . time for the sun glasses as the man himself explained, ''I used some pyrotechnics on the last Schenker tour and that was the first time I'd used so much gunpowder, it nearly burnt me every night. All I'm trying to do is frighten the audience and attempt to blow the stage up, I will eventually. The reason I do solos is because the kids like them. In fact I wanted to drop the solo when I joined Whitesnake but David said I had to do one production number.'' With the explosives, spinning mirrors, lights and flame jets and Cozy romping along to the 633 Squadron film theme music, the overall effect was (to quote the Americans) awesome.

Powell is such an individual drummer that he is impossible to ignore and his introduction into the band was probably the biggest change in feel Whitesnake had experienced so far. Reactions were varied, some feeling his arrival heralded a new era for the band, others that he was maybe too strong for them. As for the other band members, Micky Moody was relatively relaxed about it. ''I didn't notice a great change physically on-stage, though I could hear that Colin and Cozy's styles were obviously very different.''

For Jon Lord it was a different story. ''I think I felt the greatest change because I'd been playing with Ian Paice for so many years (around 14 at this stage if anyone's counting) I'd got to the point where I knew what kind of break he was going to play. Cozy is a totally different kind of drummer, far simpler I suppose. Ian is technically one of the best, I think Cozy would be the first to endorse that, yet Cozy is number one in his own field, which is about the biggest boot in the back I've ever got from a drummer.'' Cozy found he was enjoying his new position. ''For the first time in seven years I can just play drums instead of having to try and run the show. David is such a positive person, he knows exactly what he wants, I just go in and play.''

Apart from 'Crying In The Rain' the new album was largely ignored save for 'Rough And Ready', a rather weak track, plus of course the hit single which sounded rather better. Fans were divided on the new line-up, some finding the harder hitting Whitesnake a touch too close to heavy metal at times and I'd count myself among them. Others welcomed the change and the band's popularity as a live act simply went from strength to strength. Christmas was fast approaching, 'Have Yourself A Merry Whitesnake Christmas' T-shirts lobbed into the crowd proved a nice gesture and the band's undiminished drawing power was proven in Leeds where at the Queens Hall they broke the house record, promoters cramming 10,000 people into a venue designed to hold just half that number, (or a couple of dozen trams).

Back at the hotel after the show one waitress was approached by Coverdale with the age-old introduction, i.e. did she know who he was? Indoctrinated by a younger friend on the merits of a good looking long haired rock star she had seen recently, the woman made the connection. ''Yes of course sir, Ian Gillan'' . . . What happened next ain't recorded.

CHAPTER IX

1983

'SLIDE IT IN' LP
RETURN OF MURRAY
AND SYKES'S ARRIVAL

The traditional season at Hammersmith, this time four consecutive shows, ended the British tour and Whitesnake began a whistle stop European tour in mid-January. The plan was to hit as many countries as possible with two or three shows, rather than the prolonged assaults of previous years; Finland, Sweden, Germany, Switzerland and Belgium were covered inside three weeks. On the German dates they were supported by Ozzy Osbourne whose guitarist later recalled the thrill of his first European tour. "I was real excited. I asked someone in England who we would be opening for and the guy said Whitesnake." Jake Lee wondered if he was in the right place. "I never even heard of Whitesnake," he confessed.

In a complete reversal of this hit and run policy they then gave Japan saturation treatment. "This was the third time Whitesnake had been to Japan and it was by far the best tour that we've done there," Jon Lord explained on their return. "It was the longest and largest tour that anyone's done there, ever."

Whitesnake spent over two weeks in the country, playing not just the normal big urban centres but some of the smaller provincial towns, for which Jon Lord was full of praise. "There are like 2,000 seaters immaculately kept with marvellous acoustics and they really are superb gigs." The idea was to widen the appeal of the band who hadn't really broken through there to quite the extent one might have expected, while Jon also got the chance to discover what some of the Japanese keyboard manufacturers had up their sleeves.

Cozy Powell in particular was something of a superstar in his own right in the country, a reputation built on his spectacular drum routines staged during Rainbow's many visits to Japan. One manufacturer even began to market a range of Cozy Powell drumkits and sticks. As he explained, "I really make solo albums for the Japanese market, the first two went gold over there and cardboard back home."

After that they fitted in a special show in Germany to be filmed for TV before returning to the studios to begin the important task of trying to make up for the weakness of the last album. Coverdale and Galley were the prime sources of material, as Cozy Powell was quick to admit. "He's such a prolific writer he has songs coming out of his ears. The rest of us embellish what they come up with," adding that as a drummer he didn't find song-writing easy. "I much prefer to help out with arranging. It is difficult to write songs by prodding at a keyboard or humming into a tape recorder so my output is not large."

The band did two months' preliminary work at Musicland Studios where the bulk of the LP was laid down. The sessions were finished and the band returned to Britain on July 1, while Coverdale flew on to New York to do the vocals and discuss business with Geffen. They had Eddie Kramer, whose past credits included Hendrix and Traffic, doing the production work and keeping a tight reign on the schedule.

Previously with Martin Birch doing the chores, as he had for most of the Deep Purple albums, things had perhaps been allowed to pass which a new producer would automatically question. "We all felt we'd got to know Martin too well," Jon Lord explained during the sessions. "He'd become a seventh member of the band

Donington 1981.

almost. Eddie's pushed us in a direction that Martin might not have pushed us in and therefore I think he's widened the sound a bit.''

Cozy Powell's commitment in the studio led to Kramer streamlining the recording operation. ''He plays so hard that he can only do three or four tracks before he's had it for a few hours,'' said Lord. ''So if we didn't get it in three or four takes we'd have to stop for a while.'' Cozy hastened to point out that while he does need a break to recharge himself, 10 minutes or so is a more realistic time-out period. Before, with six people working at once, the chances of getting it right quickly were less than good, so this time round initial work centred on getting the drums down, along with Mel Galley's guitar and the bass part.

''Mel did most of the initial recording because he was involved in writing most of the songs, so therefore he knew them better than me,'' Micky Moody said, happy at the idea of having some of the pressure taken off his shoulders. Indeed Galley had come to the band as a prolific writer. When he auditioned in the first place he had brought along a cassette of demos which had been worked up for the next Trapeze album but left unfinished after they split. One listen to that tape convinced Coverdale and some of the material ended up on the new Whitesnake album, albeit with Coverdale's lyrics (others later ended up on the first Phenomena album).

The band felt that on previous albums the sound suffered because they had tried to cram too much on to it. ''It tended to sound a little constricted,'' Lord reasoned. ''We used to have, with Bernie and Micky, two guitarists playing the same part at the same time and then I had to get in somewhere. So we were getting this enormous amount of sound squashed into a small space.''

Word also filtered out of an alternative Whitesnake album, taped by various members of the band, with the lyrics centering not around the usual Whitesnake obsessions but rather on Jon Lord's infamous inability to get up until lunch time (which after endless phone calls I made while trying to collar him for this book I can testify to). ''I'm a hopeless insomniac, especially when recording. Then I need eight hours' sleep, so I tend to arise about two or three in the afternoon.'' The others set appropriate lyrics to well-known tunes, so 'The Lord's My Shepherd' became 'The Lord's The Organist'. Sadly, the band neglected to issue this, or other out-takes like 'Goodbye Braincells I Must Leave You'.

Other unofficial albums were beginning to appear as the band attracted the attention of bootleggers for the first time. These albums, pressed up in small numbers in Europe and Japan, varied from extremely dodgy efforts (like the recording from the band's Hammersmith gigs at the start of the year), to elaborate triple albums from Japan. With the group seemingly unwilling to issue any more official live albums, these became increasingly sought after by hard core fans. By now the group were planning their second Donington Festival appearance, this time as headliners.

Whitesnake determined to make something special of the event, turning it into something of a military campaign – which in view of conditions previous audiences had endured was probably quite apt. Backstage the whole area was decked out like a MASH unit, with military hardware decorating the field, along with sandbags, barbed wire and camp followers. Merchandise was designed to reflect the theme; sets of three badges, neatly tucked in card envelopes to resemble packets of condoms, were among items that made up Donington survival kits handed out to liggers. Two journalists were later seen heading for a secluded spot, not realising the packets didn't contain the relevant equipment.

There was even talk of stunt planes coming in but in view of the danger this was shelved. They did, however, hire every spare piece of PA in the land and cart it up there, ending up with what they reckoned was the biggest PA system ever used in the world, 100,000 watts of sound. ''Most people go in there with a couple of B&O stereo systems,'' Coverdale jibed. Two extra towers gave a quad effect during the Snakes set.

Will you be leaving the arena during Cozy's solo? queried *Kerrang!*. ''We've got a hotel booked in Leicester,'' quipped Micky Moody. ''If I can divert some of his dynamite and put it under his drum kit then he'll be leaving the arena,'' Lord suggested. The festival also marked Jon Lord's twentieth anniversary in the rock business. ''I started on August 19, 1963 with Redd Bludd's Bluesicians at the Station Hotel, Fratton, in Portsmouth. We stood in for Manfred Mann,'' he reminisced backstage. Despite all those years in the

business, he was still apprehensive. ''The sooner we go on the better. I'm really nervous – happily nervous. It gives me an edge when I get on, it vanishes the second I start playing.''

Whitesnake also influenced the bill to a large extent, making an effort to steer it away from out-and-out metal by bringing in ZZ Top and others. They warmed up for Donington with a festival in Finland and a low-key British date at Southampton Gaumont. Rehearsals at the festival site, a motor racing circuit-cum-airfield in the Midlands, augured well, except for one nervous moment when a large aircraft apparently mistook the band's enormous lighting rig for those of the nearby runway.

The show went off without a hitch. During the drum solo helicopters with searchlights added to Powell's bombastic routine, though plans for a mock battle complete with tracer bullets flying around above the crowd were, like the stunt planes, ditched due to safety problems. Not for nothing is his motto, 'If a thing's worth doing it's worth overdoing.' ''I think it'll take some beating,'' Coverdale said soon after. ''Especially as the deal I did with God to keep the rain off was so bloody expensive.'' While the BBC were refused permission to broadcast the show (having made a botch of the sound on previous occasions) the concert was filmed and although the results were far from perfect in places, it was decided to issue it as a video cassette not long afterwards.

To benefit from the publicity surrounding the festival, EMI jumped the gun and took two finished tracks from the album, 'Guilty Of Love' and 'Gambler', to make the new single. ''All the backing tracks are done, all the solos and most of the backing vocals. There's about 75 per cent of David's vocals still to go on and then the mixing,'' Jon explained when asked why the LP wasn't yet out. In the event, these were to be the only numbers from the Eddie Kramer sessions to see the light of day. When the single began to take off, footage from festival rehearsals was used to make a promo for it.

After the noise of Donington had died away the band flew out for dates in Europe. The Monsters Of Rock banner had by this time been stretched to cover several major festivals there, with Meatloaf and other bands, although Whitesnake also gigged on their own. It was during this tour that Thin Lizzy with John Sykes on guitar supported Whitesnake on some shows.

Micky Moody was by this time determined to leave once the tour ended. His initial enthusiasm had quickly

Headliners at Donington, 1981.

waned. ''I wasn't enjoying being on the road but musically I wasn't enjoying it either. It had become heavier. I love Cozy but the flames and explosions every night, it really was like an act, like a circus.'' Moody missed the old atmosphere and didn't like Coverdale's way of running the group now that he was effectively in charge. He even suggested to the band that they bring in

Following the tour the others returned to Musicland to finish work on the album. By this time rumours that all was not well within the band were circulating widely. As far back as March, sources close to the group indicated that changes would be made once touring commitments had been fulfilled. Coverdale approached John Sykes, and he was auditioned at Musicland playing along to some of the album backing tracks. He was in two minds whether to accept or not, having made plans with Phil Lynott to form a new band after Thin Lizzy's last tour – indeed the pair of them had already done a few low-key shows in Scandinavia. In the end he accepted Coverdale's offer. It was some time before Lynott wanted to hear the name Whitesnake again.

By this time Coverdale had also come to the conclusion that Kramer's production work wasn't what he was after. Kramer was relieved of the job and Martin Birch was persuaded to do a salvage job yet again. No sooner had Coverdale begun laying the vocals down than he collapsed in the studio through exhaustion and it was to be a fortnight before he could resume work. "This album had to be done right because I've made too many excuses for the last album," he told one journalist. With Moody out, the next to jump overboard was Colin Hodgkinson. He hadn't been fitting in well socially or musically, and Cozy in particular had problems working with him in the studio. He stormed out of the drum booth at one session with a snappy, "Let me introduce myself, I'm the drummer, let's get together sometime."

On December 1, Neil Murray was asked to audition for the band once more. As far back as Donington he'd realised something was in the air when Whitesnake's road manager asked him whether he was contracted to Gary Moore or not. He wasn't. In fact while it had been going well on the road, Murray felt more like a session player when it came to recording, so he was happy to move on. "I think he wasn't really happy playing this kind of music any more basically," Moore commented. "He was getting a bit pissed off, plus he had a bit of a run-in with the producer."

The band could hardly afford another protracted round of personnel changes of the kind which had taken them off the road for nearly a year in 1982, which is why this time round the prospective candidates were approached well in advance. In a fit of optimism a British tour through December was announced in October but with the album delays – Coverdale finally finished work in late November – they realised it would

John Sykes to replace him. The final straw came when, seated in a hotel with Galley and Sykes after one show, Coverdale told him off for playing with his back to the audience. If Moody had entertained any doubts about leaving, that ended them. After the final show he called everyone up to his room and told them he was leaving. This time his departure was for good.

John Sykes and amplifier collection, 1984.

be impossible to get the show worked up in the time available, so the gigs were rescheduled for February and March.

As before, the papers were told little of what was going on and prospective guitarists were given a phone number in the papers but John Sykes was never under any real threat. By mid-December *Sounds* had got hold of the story and his appointment was confirmed.

John Sykes was born in the UK, but at 14 moved to Spain where his parents owned a club. With nothing to do – he didn't speak Spanish – he took up guitar. "I was listening to people like Eric Clapton and Johnny Winter and then I got into Blackmore, 'Highway Star' and all that."

Sykes was on the dole when the family returned from Spain and he moved up to Blackpool with them. There he teamed up with a local band called Streetfighter. Answering an advert in *Melody Maker* not long afterwards he found himself auditioning for and joining The Tigers Of Pan Tang. He did two albums for them when Ozzy Osbourne called to offer him the rest of his US tour as replacement for Randy Rhoads who was killed in a flying accident. Ozzie had recruited

Bernie Torme for a couple of shows but he wasn't fitting in. After the initial offer though, Sykes heard no more and in the end didn't do the tour.

Instead he went off and did a solo single with Phil Lynott and a couple of guys from Thin Lizzy. Osbourne eventually gave him an audition for his group but by then Lynott had offered him a job in Thin Lizzy which he accepted at once, playing on their 'Thunder And Lightning' album and the subsequent tour.

It was on this tour that Coverdale saw the young guitarist and made tentative enquiries as to his working in Whitesnake. At first it seemed as if the band's history of releasing a new album with a line-up different from that in the band would be repeated, but this time there was a twist to the story. Over in America Geffen took one listen to the Martin Birch produced version of the new album, now titled 'Slide It In', and decided they were unhappy with it. They demanded a remix before they would consider issuing it in America and Coverdale was persuaded to agree.

CHAPTER X

1984-1985

'SLIDE IT IN'
TO 'ROCK IN RIO'

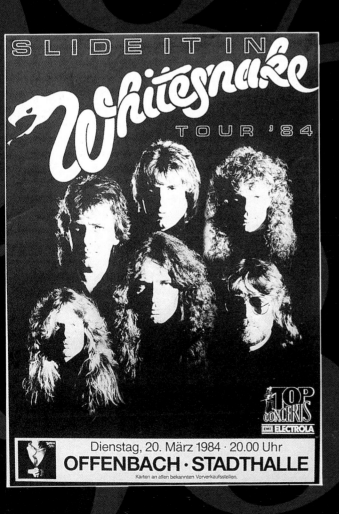

SLIDE IT IN
Whitesnake
TOUR '84

TOP CONCERTS
EMI ELECTROLA

Dienstag, 20. März 1984 · 20.00 Uhr
OFFENBACH·STADTHALLE
Karten an allen bekannten Vorverkaufsstellen.

Donington 1981.

While the new album 'Slide It In' came out in Europe in January and the new line-up gathered in London for group photos, Geffen knocked the tapes into shape for America with Keith Olsen, the man behind recent production successes for Foreigner and Pat Benatar. As it was being remixed anyhow they decided to bring the album line-up back up to date by having Sykes and Murray flown out to the Goodnight Studios in LA to redo the guitar and bass. Murray managed to re-record all the bass but with time short and Olsen taken ill, Sykes wasn't able to redo all the guitar work, so the American edition still has Micky Moody's licks in places.

'Slide It In' entered the British charts at number nine, just as the band began two weeks of intensive rehearsals before their first shows in Ireland. As they did so cassettes of the Geffen remix reached the band. It had originally been agreed that they would do a couple of remixes but in the end only one turned up and Whitesnake were unimpressed to say the least. An Irish journalist caught the brunt of their reactions. "Mel Galley threw the cassette against the wall. 'It sucks as far as I'm concerned and if that goes out I'm not gonna be with Geffen any more'." Coverdale unburdened himself after two successful gigs in Dublin. "It's dynamically dull, it's lost its British bollocks," he said.

Geffen, however, were sure they were on the right lines and over the weeks the others came round to the extent that eventually Coverdale would never play the European version. It was something of a ritual that Coverdale used to psyche himself up by having tapes of the band blasting out of his dressing room, something the others didn't always appreciate. "We couldn't stand

to hear them over and over like that," Neil Murray said.

A general loathing for much of the AOR style favoured by many American bands was probably one reason for the initial dislike, a kind of British prejudice at the perceived inability of Americans to handle real rock music unless it was blanded out. Certainly many fans felt that if America couldn't take Whitesnake as they were, then hard luck. In the papers the band were at pains to play the remix down, especially as it might look as if they'd originally put out something with which they were less than happy. I don't think anyone thought they had but when imports of the US version reached these shores our complacency was in for a severe shock for it was that much better.

Maybe some of the initial anger within the band stemmed from the realisation that here at last was the sound they'd been after for so long and if they had achieved this result before, then maybe American success wouldn't have eluded them for so long. Yet it had been brought about with only slight adjustments to the sound, touches which only a producer could explain. The days of getting a good sound and then mixing it were clearly no longer enough. The main impact came on the first side, with the tracks rearranged to produce a hard hitting sequence, leaving the lesser cuts for the second side.

Subtle it ain't, but lyrics aside, on the track 'Slide It In' the modern streamlined Whitesnake sound of today is clearly evident. Powell and Murray unable to play well together? Coverdale's fears were unfounded, they don't come much harder than this. The vocals were lifted up over the sound, little hiccups in some numbers had been ironed out, while what would have been tinny

backing vocals on earlier efforts were lifted to a full blown vocal choir.

Galley's first writing credit came with the magnificent 'Love Ain't No Stranger' and it still amazes me that tracks like this and 'Slow An' Easy' didn't break the band there and then. 'Gambler' closed the first side, the third vinyl version of the song and one of the few tracks where Jon Lord could be heard to any great effect. This was one of those tracks originally put together by Trapeze, while the lighter 'Standing In The Shadows' was a number Coverdale originally worked out with MSG in mind a couple of years before.

While arguments about the remix continued and imports did healthy business, the rest of the tour motored along; again a mixture of the smaller halls and some biggies. For the first time since the band had formed, Hammersmith Odeon was passed over in favour of Wembley, such was the demand for tickets, although in the end the band were so nervous that it wasn't one of their better shows. Mel Galley found it hard to take some of the pomp and ceremony which went with the group seriously. "I got to Wembley for the soundcheck and Sykes had been on to Marshall and he must have had six or eight 100 watt stacks with I don't know how many amps. He wanted them all switched on as well so the lights were on but he only used like two of the speakers.'' Galley draped a screen over his own gear and brought out his practise amp, intending to do the show with that.

Leeds Queens Hall were finally caught out with the serious overcrowding at rock gigs. With over five thousand tickets already sold, the local council slapped a temporary limit of just over 4,000. To get over the problem the band gave up their rest day to play a second night at the venue. Along with the fans, most of the city council's licensing committee went along as well to see for themselves the problems at the hall. The local papers loved it. 'Councillors roll to rock concert', screamed the headline.

Over in Liverpool at the Royal Court, nobody seemed to want to turn on the heating. Coverdale's breath condensed in the air because it was so cold at the start of the show, yet over in Cardiff Cozy Powell's pyrotechnics raised the temperature so much they set off the venue's fire alarms.

Despite such problems, the UK tour went so well that after a fortnight in Germany (with the last few dates pulled to allow Coverdale's voice to recover) they slotted in some more British gigs in early April (putting back the Japanese tour to do so), then flew back out from Manchester to play the cancelled German gigs.

With a day off prior to the first gig in Ludwigshafen, the band decided to relax at a local funfair. Larking around on the way back Galley and Sykes decided to make it back to the hotel the hard way, leaping over parked cars. Galley managed to trip and Sykes followed him over, landing straight on his arm. A broken arm naturally put him out of action but having already delayed the tour once they decided to complete the dates as a five-piece.

"We were thrown in at the deep end," Coverdale commented in one interview. "Because of a dreadful accident that I wouldn't wish on my worst enemy. We agreed to finish the tour as a five-piece. They were the most exciting shows I'd ever done. It was the first time that Whitesnake had ever really felt like a group." Ironically Jon Lord, who had been fed up earlier in the tour when he'd discovered Cozy was being paid twice as much as he was, felt much happier during the five shows than he'd done for a long time. With only one guitarist he was able to contribute much more to the overall sound. To a large extent it was immaterial.

On April 16 the band finished the tour with a weird Swedish TV set, Whitesnake playing to a dinner suited seated audience in between classical flautists and God knows what. Four of them flew home, while Jon Lord left for America and a meeting with Ritchie Blackmore, Ian Paice, Ian Gillan and Roger Glover. He knew Whitesnake weren't far off making it really big. "It wasn't easy for me to leave Whitesnake, they're on the verge of becoming a major international band." The chance to complete unfinished business with Deep Purple would have been hard to resist. Sykes was less kind. "I think the changes are certainly for the better, that old Hammond sound dated the stuff by about 15 years anyway."

Whitesnake were now without a keyboard player. A further blow came when it was discovered that after Galley's accident, when the hospital had bound his bones with a metal plate, a virus had set in. "It ate away the nerves from the hand right up to the bass of the skull. By the time they'd found out what the trouble was, I'd lost the use of my wrist, my arm, everything, and I couldn't play." He would be out of action for much longer than they'd anticipated, indeed specialists were sceptical about his ever playing again. Whitesnake kept his wages going for the time being and carried on working as a four-piece.

Over in the States 'Slide It In' was beginning to justify Geffen's faith in the band and their insistence on the remix, while the single 'Slow An' Easy' was also showing promise. The quartet nipped down to the Brixton Academy in early May to shoot a video for it which was shipped over for heavy rotation on MTV. Seeing it, Geffen were at once impressed by the look of the band. Rather than try and replace Jon Lord they opted instead for an off-stage keyboard role and hired Richard Bailey for the time being.

It was in this form that they headlined a two-day festival in Switzerland on July 1, 1984 before heading out to America and the start of a long haul to try and build on the album's early sales. When Whitesnake headlined at Donington the previous year, Coverdale had personally invited Dio to share the bill. Now Dio took the opportunity to repay that by offering Whitesnake the support slot on their US tour. It was a chaotic few weeks, Coverdale claiming that the only way he knew where they were playing from one night to the next was by reading the T-shirts. The set was squeezed to around half an hour as they were having to make room for a third act at most shows.

"Good evening, we're a bunch of sleaze buckets from London," was Coverdale's favourite introduction for a band that was still an unknown quantity to many of the crowds. They performed tracks off 'Slide It In'

Jon Lord considers his future career after the last Whitesnake show, Stockholm, April 1984.

along with 'Ready An' Willing', keyboards man Richard Bailey hidden behind a curtain. "We have a side order of keyboards. He's not sleazy enough just yet to be seen on stage," Coverdale explained.

As the tour progressed Coverdale realised that Sykes was handling things more than adequately on his own. "I'm anticipating total involvement from Sykes and we'll be working 50/50. That'll be the first time really that I ever had a 50/50 collaboration with anybody as far as writing goes, no matter what former members of Whitesnake say." In fact Sykes had shrewdly insisted on such a split, realising his worth to the band.

After a month on the road, the band left the tour to fly out to Japan for some massive festival dates held under the banner of Super Rock '84. Whitesnake were headlining, alternating with MSG on a bill that also included The Scorpions, Anvil and Bon Jovi. For once the switching of headliners was more than just an ego boost to whoever topped. The hot and humid conditions made playing earlier in the day particularly uncomfortable, while the early end to shows in Japan (where rock gigs always end by 8.30pm) meant most groups were playing in bright sun, so lights were often a waste of time. Souvenir videos of the shows were released soon after in Japan.

Back home Mel Galley's fate as a performing member of Whitesnake was sealed when Coverdale saw the weird contraption strapped to his arm. A specially designed brace replaced the missing nerves in his arm and enabled him to start playing once more. "You can't play in the band with that on," he told Galley. "You'll look like a spastic." Words Galley is unlikely to forget

KLOS 95½ welcomes

QUIET RIOT

with Special Guest

WHITE SNAKE

and Special Added Attraction

ARMORED SAINT

Sunday 7:00 P.M.

Reserved: $16.00*/$14.00*
Meadows/Lawn: $9.50*

ON SALE MONDAY 10AM

SEPTEMBER

30

but which actually spurred him on to prove Coverdale wrong, as his subsequent involvement with the Phenomena project and later the band MGM did just that.

Back in the USA, Geffen arranged for another promo video, this time for 'Love Ain't No Stranger', which they shot in Hollywood, with Rudy Sarzo's girlfriend providing linking footage between shots of the band on-stage. Despite 22 takes for the on-stage sequences they still managed to get the footage out of sync. The band were to spend almost the rest of the year on the road in the States. Whitesnake took second billing to Quiet Riot and it began to pay off, with 'Slide It In' edging into the US charts.

For Quiet Riot's Kevin DuBrow, having Whitesnake opening for his band was something of a dream come true as he had been a fan of Coverdale for many years. "The reason for our lack of touring over here is twofold," Coverdale found himself explaining to the press. "One is that over the years our past record companies never promoted us properly. They were waiting for the public to demand that we were brought over to tour." A crazy situation given that the band's reputation as a live act across Europe far outweighed their track record on vinyl. "The other reason is that we were having so much success in Europe that there wasn't really a reason for us to stretch out to America. Why should we come here spending years as an opening act when we could have stayed close to home and headlined?" Now Coverdale saw commercial and artistic survival hinging on the band breaking America.

Interviewers who raised the subject of the Deep Purple reunion were generally given short shrift, but when one idiot asked him what he had contributed to the reunion, a suitably irritated Coverdale snapped back "Jon Lord". Twelve weeks on the road, travelling in humid coaches they nicknamed Pizza Ovens, began to tell on Whitesnake and once again friction between the members of the band started to surface. Money problems were at the root of it all. Sykes, together with Powell (never happy when everything is running smoothly) decided to put to David the idea of a four-way split to make things more democratic. At a meeting in December to try and sort this out it was clear that nothing of the sort was going to happen. Cozy Powell decided enough was enough and handed in his notice. Whitesnake decided to quit the tour in any case, as Quiet Riot were having difficulty in pulling crowds as they reached the East Coast, often having to switch venues to avoid large empty halls. "We did get sick of the claustrophobic surroundings of the tour bus and the incessant moaning of our Tennessee bus driver. The noise and distractions such as people playing music or videos made it not the ideal way of recuperating after the shows," Neil Murray commented later.

It had indeed been a long hard slog but when it came to an end on December 22 they had the satisfaction of knowing that 'Slide It In' had shifted over 300,000 copies and at last there were some Americans who knew who they were. Ironically Geffen were later to

admit they hadn't really pushed the album as hard as they could have done in the latter stages of the tour. If they had done so the chances are fairly strong that it would have broken the band that year.

After Christmas the band flew down to the Rock In Rio festival in Brazil where they played two shows during the 10-day event, the first supporting Queen and Iron Maiden, the second opening for The Scorpions and Ozzy Osbourne. Though nobody knew it at the time these were to be the last Whitesnake shows for almost three years. Voted sex object of the festival by the audience and with local companies interested in him for promotional purposes, Coverdale was in a buoyant mood as he looked forward to 1985. Despite the stomach illnesses caused by the water supply, conditions were good and away from the shows the bands relaxed.

John Sykes met up with Tommy Aldridge, playing his last show with Ozzy Osbourne. Aldridge being his favourite drummer, he made strenuous efforts to get him in to Whitesnake there and then but Coverdale wasn't sure, preferring to look instead for an English drummer. Had he realised just how long it was going to take to try and find one, he might have changed his mind.

CHAPTER XI

February 1985 -
early 1987

THE NEW ALBUM AND LINE-UP

While Cozy Powell teamed up with Keith Emerson and Greg Lake for the ill-fated ELP reunion in which Carl Palmer had refused to get involved, Whitesnake began planning the next album, with talk of a tour with The Scorpions once it was finished. "Being a big success elsewhere, it's awfully hard to slog around the clubs in the US," Neil spoke wearily at the thought. "When other bands – like Iron Maiden – are coming out of nowhere and taking on the world it's all the more tough. It's not always fun going back to the beginning again and having to start over."

John Sykes and Neil Murray spent some time during February up at Sykes' studio in Blackpool, the wind-swept resort on the west coast of England, hardly the most glamorous place to begin what was to become a mega platinum album. EMI, anxious at the band's non-appearance here for some considerable time, kept the pot boiling by issuing a couple of US mixed tracks as a single in January, following this with a picture disc album of the complete US mix of 'Slide It In' a couple of months later. That the band were looking for a drummer became gossip in many of the music papers and eventually a contact phone number for prospective skin-bashers was published. It was left to Neil Murray to sift through the cassettes, though nothing emerged that set his heart racing. While he busied himself mailing out polite rejection slips, John Sykes joined David at a villa in the south of France to continue work on the new material.

Already he and Coverdale were having serious differences of opinion over the material and at one point Sykes was on the verge of upping to form a new band altogether. Eventually he came round and along with Neil Murray began taping demos of the material back in Blackpool during June. Finally at the end of the month the pair left for the sunnier climes of Los Angeles where Coverdale had set up camp and was to remain from now on.

They began serious rehearsals and in between sessions started at last to audition drummers. In the end about a dozen hopefuls were brought in, including Quiet Riot's Frankie Banali, which didn't go down too well with them. Tommy Aldridge and Rudy Sarzo, busy launching their band Driver, were approached to do the album too. "Rudy and I really wanted to give Driver a shot at recording, we wanted to see what we could come up with on our own. Boy, that was one great career move," Aldridge explained when asked why they'd turned it down.

Neil Murray only later found out about the approach to Sarzo. It wasn't until August that Aynsley Dunbar was auditioned. "We spent about £85,000 auditioning 60 drummers who couldn't drive a truck let alone a fucking band," Coverdale was moved to say after finally finding Dunbar.

In the early sixties Aynsley Dunbar was one of many musicians to emerge from Liverpool where he was widely regarded as one of the best Merseybeat drummers. Leaving The Mojos he moved down to London in 1966 for spells with Jeff Beck and John Mayall's Bluesbreakers before forming his own band, Aynsley Dunbar's Retaliation, turning down offers to join The New Yardbirds, better known as Led Zeppelin, to stick with it. As the seventies dawned, Dunbar left for America where he was signed up by Frank Zappa for

Cozy Powell, John Sykes and Neil Murray, Japanese tour, 1984.

Dear

Thank you for your recent application for the vacant position of drummer with Whitesnake.

It is with regret that I inform you your application has been unsuccessful.

On behalf of the band, I would like to thank you for your support and interest and wish you every success in your future career.

All the best

five albums, after which he did sessions for many of the best known rock acts around, including David Bowie, Sammy Hagar, Lou Reed and Nils Lofgren, before joining Journey in 1974 and going from there to The Starship. For two years prior to auditioning for Whitesnake, Dunbar had been doing lucrative session work.

Now back to full strength, more problems loomed when nobody could agree on a producer. None of the band were keen on getting Keith Olsen back in, despite his previous work remixing 'Slide It In'. After a long debate they plumped for Mike Stone, the man behind Journey and Asia's production. During this time, Sykes did some rehearsing for David Lee Roth and is credited on his first album although he didn't join him in the studio. At long last Whitesnake arrived at Little Mountain studios in Vancouver (chosen after good reports from people like Bon Jovi) at the back end of September and work on recording began.

Even now problems began to arise. Dunbar, used to working as a session player, hadn't been with the band long enough to feel or establish himself as a full member. Thus when the others, especially John Sykes who has always been something of a perfectionist in the studio, began to tell him how to approach each little bit, he did as he was asked. The end results were great drum tracks but the effect was to prolong the sessions on in to December. Neil Murray's old acquaintance Don Airey was flown over to lay down keyboard parts which he did with the efficiency of an old hand, taking just five days to do so. More delays caused by Sykes's tonsillitis delayed work and it wasn't until the end of December that the backings were more or less completed.

"It took to the end of the year. At this point Mike Stone had to start rescheduling everything and was getting pretty fed up. In January John redid all the guitar backings and David started doing some vocals and it all became a real nightmare," Neil Murray recalled. Phil Lynott had been trying to lure Sykes back to a reformed Thin Lizzy but instead Sykes found himself flying back from America to attend Lynott's funeral and spend time with his relatives.

Top: Coverdale and Sykes turn to in-house catering during the band's lay-off!
Bottom: Backstage during Quiet Riot tour. *(L–R)* Off stage keyboard player Richard Bailey, Rudy Sarzo, David Coverdale & Cozy Powell.

John Sykes practising guitar aerobics, Stockholm, April 1984.

Once this unavoidable delay was over, Coverdale began recording the lead vocals back up in Canada. During sessions in March he decided the results were not as good as they should have been. "I started to sound very nasal. I sang out of tune from beginning to end, I was physically exhausted by it. I had temple pains like migraine, I was scared to death." Doctors were consulted and he was told it was nothing more than a serious cold. "I sounded like Peter Lorre," he later joked but at the time it was hardly a laughing matter.

By April things reached a crisis point. Mike Stone had more or less refused to carry on until he had vocals to work to. Coverdale saw another specialist and a correct diagnosis was obtained. "He said it was the worst sinus infection he'd ever seen." He was told that it would need surgery to cure. Coverdale took a course of antibiotics, hoping to recover enough to finish the album off before an operation became necessary, or at least get some guide vocals down. "We immediately booked Compass Point Studios in the Bahamas," Coverdale explained, but although he had been led to believe the infection had been halted, a fortnight in the studio produced nothing with which he was happy. At this point Mike Stone, unhappy at being tied up for so long on the project, suggested that Coverdale get someone else in to do the vocals so he could get on with the rest of the production. Perhaps not surprisingly Stone and Coverdale's working arrangements finished at that point.

Pressure was also being exerted from elsewhere; that same month Aynsley Dunbar and Neil Murray were laid off as Geffen decided to stop paying wages. Expenses for studio work would still be forthcoming but this would apply mainly to Coverdale and Sykes. Finally Coverdale went in for an operation after making one last attempt at a rough vocal so that during the interim period John Sykes could at least have something to work around. Stone gave it a bash but during May at Phase One Studio in Toronto with Sykes laying down further guitar parts, he gave up and refused to carry on until the vocals were laid down. Aynsley disappeared and Neil Murray recalled. "If we'd done the album and gone out on the road in 1986 then he would probably have stayed in the band but he couldn't afford to wait around with no money coming in."

Murray was told, much as he had been back in 1982, that if he needed to put in time with another band to keep himself going then that was fine. However, few bands were interested in a bassist who was liable to be called up at any moment to rejoin another group and in the end, with no wage and no royalties coming in off any of the earlier Whitesnake albums, he resorted to selling off his equipment and bass guitars to make ends meet.

Even after the operation it took some time for Coverdale to get over the problems his absence from the studio had caused. "I had some troubles with my throat. At first I believed there was something physically wrong with my voice. It got to the point where I began developing a mental block towards singing. I knew I wasn't really having any physical problems." For a time, Coverdale faced a psychological barrier which had to be overcome in order to see the album through. After recovering physically from his operation, which added another two months to the album's gestation period, Coverdale took some vocal lessons for the first time in his life. His tutor was a Jewish Cantor, Nathan Lam, who took Coverdale through basic singing exercises and scales.

"I'd drive down from the Jewish temple in LA feeling full of it, the exercises not only helped my singing but my breathing as well," he said afterwards. In June he returned to the studio to try out the results of this tuition. "My first reaction was to go back and work with someone I knew could get the best out of me. That man was Martin Birch but to be honest Martin and I haven't been getting along that well in recent years so that part of my plan went awry. The next person I could think of was Ron Nevison."

With Nevison at the helm he laid down a few vocal tracks. Happy with the results, the production sound was a little too smooth for him and so Coverdale got back in touch with Keith Olsen. "He said he'd be delighted to work on the album." So Coverdale set up shop in Goodnight Studios in LA and got back into the swing of things in a serious way. Initially nervous, Olsen tricked him into doing a take of 'Still Of The Night' ostensibly as a practise run, while he actually let the tapes roll in order to show Coverdale that he really had come out of the nightmare.

The problem well and truly laid to rest, Coverdale did the finished vocals during August, September and October. John Sykes was also on hand, helping out with the backing vocals. Back home Neil Murray took up an offer from Bernie Marsden and Mel Galley to join a group they were forming. Christened MGM after the initials of their surnames, he did so on the understanding that he was still obligated to Whitesnake.

In LA Coverdale and Sykes were still having difficulties getting along with one another; rows about the wisdom of redoing old Whitesnake tracks and who would mix the album continued to make life difficult for all concerned. Sykes bowed to Coverdale's choice of producer for the vocals but was himself determined

John Sykes and Mel Galley, Germany, just prior to Mel's accident.

John Sykes, Japan, July 1984.

Newcomer Adrian Vandenberg, ace Dutch guitarist.

to ensure his guitar work remained under the guidance of Mike Stone. Sykes flew back to London in October where he and Murray went into the studio with Stone to add the last few guitar solos and redo a few bass parts, Sykes having discovered to his horror that some of his guitar had disappeared from the tapes over the summer.

These long running niggles finally came to a head in December. Stone decided that after nearly two years' work he didn't want to prolong his involvement. Geffen quickly brought back Keith Olsen and he and David Coverdale began the mixing at Goodnight in December. Sykes, excluded from the mixing and convinced that all his hard work was in jeopardy, flew out to LA unannounced to confront Coverdale.

The result of this row was Sykes' departure from the outfit post-haste; this time he would not return. "We put together a strong unit that recorded this album, but we had some problems, especially Sykes and myself. He's a brilliant guitarist but I'm too old to be a baby sitter, so we went our separate ways – which was probably best for everyone," said Coverdale.

To all intents and purposes Whitesnake were no longer a band as 1987 rolled round, and during February Neil Murray heard via a journalist at *Kerrang!* that his services would no longer be required. Geffen, anxious to wind up the album as quickly as possible, gathered an *ad hoc* unit to shoot a couple of videos, using people they and Coverdale had seen or heard over the years. John Kalodner at Geffen knew guitarist Vivian Campbell from tapes of a trio called Trinity. While Kalodner admired Campbell's playing he felt Trinity wasn't a suitable vehicle for his style. "He said 'This isn't for you, get back in a hard rock band.' He even tried putting a project together for me with Carl Palmer and Joe Lynn Turner. Eventually he called about Whitesnake's video," Campbell recalled.

Irish born and bred, he had been catapulted to the top of the rock scene when he joined Ronnie James Dio's band, formed after Dio quit Blackmore's

Rainbow. It was with Dio that Campbell's guitar work was first brought to the attention of most rock fans but life in the band wasn't all it might have been, ruled over as it was by Ronnie and his wife and manager Wendy. In his spare moments Campbell began working with Trinity to find ways to express himself outside the confines of Dio. Then in 1986 Ronnie fired Campbell. "It was a very bad year for me. I never wanted to leave Dio but I guess in the back of my mind I knew what would eventually happen."

In one of those strange moments of rock and roll musical chairs which have been a hallmark of the Whitesnake story, Campbell was contacted by Tommy Aldridge as soon as the Dio gig ended, with an offer to join Driver alongside Rudy Sarzo. They were short of a guitarist as their man Craig Goldie had just quit – to go and join Dio. Since Driver were at that time something of an unknown quantity Campbell decided to turn Trinity into a full-time project but it was a struggle from start to finish, especially financially. "We ran up against every conceivable problem. When David called I had a couple of other offers as well. The other projects were 'if and maybe'. I hadn't toured in so long and Trinity drained me because it was a self-financed project."

Campbell was using cash he'd saved up during Dio to fund it all, hoping to survive long enough to record the material he'd written outside Dio. Things went from bad to worse and when Geffen phoned he decided to accept Coverdale's offer to do the video shoot in the hopes that it might lead to a full-time job, though Coverdale said nothing to begin with. "He didn't make an offer, he was very very vague waiting to see how these people worked together."

"These people" were all approached in a similar fashion. Drummer Tommy Aldridge and bassist Rudy Sarzo had been working together for a time. "Rudy and I released the Driver album on an independent label called Shrapnel Records in 1987 and were trying for a major deal."

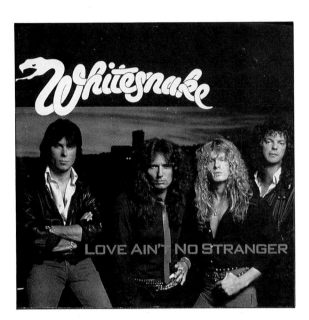

Below: The humidity starts to take its toll in Japan, July 1984.

Below: Neil Murray makes sure he is still in the band before signing autographs.

The pair had also done a project called NRG together and this too was close to gaining a deal for them. The Driver album was issued in Japan and did fairly well but the band was costing a lot of money to keep going. "I was doing drum clinics for Yamaha," explained Tommy Aldridge. "Which is how I was paying my bills. Rudy and I spent a lot trying to put a band together, flying people in to audition, paying for rehearsal time." Their main stumbling block was in finding a suitable singer, so in a sense Coverdale's phone call came at an opportune moment. "He got the band he needed, we got the vocalist we were looking for," Aldridge reasoned.

One thing is certain, when the pair saw the personnel assembled for the video, they were both convinced it would turn into a full-time project. "I looked around the room and said 'This is the band'," Rudy Sarzo recalled of that first meeting. Campbell felt the same way. "From the first moment there was a great feeling, very very strong. Everyone was saying, 'This could be one hell of a group if it happens'."

Aldridge's past credits ran back to 1970 when he joined Black Oak Arkansas at the age of 18. He spent six years with them but the split was less than amicable and for a year after leaving he was unable to record or join a band. When he did take up the sticks again it was to start a four-year stint with Pat Travers, time wasted to some extent when the group folded on the verge of breaking through. Aldridge returned to sessions and was in London helping Gary Moore out when Ozzy Osbourne asked him to join his band, recalling Aldridge from way back when Black Oak Arkansas opened for Sabbath on a British concert tour. It was with Ozzy's band that Aldridge found Rudy Sarzo on bass and together they formed Driver with guitarist Tony McAlpine.

Rudy Sarzo, born in Cuba during the fifties, adopted bass seriously as a career in the seventies. "I lived a very sheltered life, mainly because I was in Miami and my parents were Cuban which meant they had this Latin type of attitude towards the world." When he did break out it was to become a founder member of Quiet Riot and he spent several years with them off and on before leaving amid a certain amount of acrimony. The band had accused Sarzo of almost taking over the band on-stage. "Rudy was a gunslinger, it was the Rudy Sarzo Show not Quiet Riot," drummer Frankie Banali had commented not long after Sarzo's departure. "I always believed in going for the gusto on-stage and if you call that being a gunslinger, fine. I was always very professional and only cared about putting on a great show."

Whitesnake opened for Quiet Riot in 1984 in America and it was there that Sarzo first met Coverdale, though he admits he didn't mix with him much and didn't know what to make of the situation. "He seemed to be spending most of his time arguing with John Sykes. They were brilliant on-stage but I didn't know how stable the group was, I didn't know if I wanted to get involved with another band which seemed to have a lot of conflict going on. David spoke to me about working with him during that tour. I was aware that personnel problems were holding him up. Geffen called me up and asked if I wanted to appear in the 'Still Of The Night' video, I didn't know that he had

The new look is complete, Whitesnake's rebirth, 1987. Campbell, Aldridge, Vandenberg, Coverdale and Sarzo.

also contacted all the other guys. Coverdale was behind it all. Once we got together we immediately saw the potential this line-up had. It only took me 24 hours after that video was finished to know that I wanted to be part of what was going on with Whitesnake.'' The remaining piece of the jigsaw expressed similar enthusiasm.

"Whitesnake had such a great line-up I couldn't resist,'' said Dutchman Adrian Vandenberg, who had actually been in touch with Coverdale several times over the years while fronting a successful band under his own name. He had been in the running for Whitesnake back in 1983 before Sykes joined the band. "He heard the first Vandenberg album and called me. David had been particularly impressed with a track on that album called 'Burning Heart'.''

Indeed he had. "I think his writing is very much in tune with what I do, that could have been my song,'' Coverdale enthused. "We met when Whitesnake played Holland. He asked me to join him four or five times but I wanted my own project because Whitesnake's line-up was always changing. This time I felt it was right because I was having difficulties finding inspiration continuing with Vandenberg.'' He had done well to get the group as far as he had. Holland has remained something of a rock 'n' roll backwater. "Contracts are hard to obtain because of controls on radio and the market. Sales of 8,000 are considered outstanding, we sold 25,000 records there and that's

a lot, AC/DC albums sell half that number.''

Vandenberg was actually the first of the new Whitesnake members to record with the group. At the behest of Geffen, convinced that it was hit material, another take of 'Here I Go Again' was laid down, this time using musicians on a session basis: the rhythm section from Heart – Mark Andes on bass and Denny Carmassi on drums – plus Alan Pasqua on keyboards with Dan Huff and Adrian Vandenberg on guitar (though confusingly the video for this hit version used the album take). "I remember hearing the single all the time in British clubs and I thought it was incredible. I would never have dreamed that four years later I would re-record the song with David and it would be a hit all over again,'' Vandenberg told someone after the session.

Even at this point Coverdale was still making up his mind about a band. "After waiting so long to actually get this album out I don't want to be pushed in to making irrational decisions,'' he told a reporter a couple of days after making the video. "If I involve myself with people I want to be able to guarantee them that I will be able to take care of them. That of course will be dictated by the success of the album. The video shoot was a treat, everybody got on great. I was thinking of changing the name of the band to The League Of Nations, we had a Dutchman, an Irishman, a Cuban, a Texan and an Englishman. I understand Tommy and Rudy have just got a deal together for a new album, who knows?'' he concluded mysteriously.

XII

1987 - 1988

'WHITESNAKE 1987', THE NEW ALBUM TO 1988

Previous Page: The new line-up hit the road, 1987.

Remington lady-shave? No way! US tour 1987.

With the videos in the can, all that remained was for Coverdale and Geffen to sit back and wait nervously to see how the album would fare. While he shared the enthusiasm felt by the band that shot the video, Coverdale certainly wasn't going to spoil it all by rushing into anything.

"It's been an extraordinarily expensive two-and-a-half years. At this point in time if I involve myself with people I want to be able to guarantee them that I will be able to take care of them. That of course will be dictated by the success of the album. There are certain things on the boiler as we speak," he hinted to the reporter from one magazine. "If that happens I'll form a band within five minutes." If the two-and-a-half year lay-off had taught him anything, it was to take things as they come.

Time was spent re-editing the video. "I wasn't happy with the way I looked, so I had a lot of my scenes edited out," Coverdale explained. Indeed he confessed to a certain amount of dislike for the now popular 'story line' MTV led videos as compared to live 'in concert' footage the band had been doing in the past. "The process did seem a bit stiff and artificial to one who grew up in a different era. We spent 25 hours straight in front of the camera." If you watch the video for 'Still Of The Night' very carefully, in particular the garage floor shot, you will notice that the cracks in the concrete match those on the album sleeve exactly. Indeed, the album cover was curiously devoid of Whitesnake's usual trademarks when it reached the stores in April. Leaving MTV to take care of the promotion chores at home, Coverdale returned to Europe for a round of radio and press interviews.

Issued in April, 'Whitesnake '87' (as it is generally referred to) came as something of a shock to people who knew the band from past albums. Gone were the ramshackle production jobs, replaced by a powerful American sounding wall of sound, cyclonic guitar runs and all. Reviewers were quick to point out that underneath this impressive studio work the material was perhaps not always what it might have been. Whitesnake's 'Saints An' Sinners' album, as we've seen, had never even been issued in America, yet two of the new album's strongest tracks were re-recorded versions of tunes which had first surfaced on that early LP. For this reason the American and European versions of the album were varied to avoid giving fans back home too many revamped oldies.

On tracks like 'Give Me All Your Love' the Whitesnake sound of old is still very much in evidence, especially Neil Murray's bubbling bass lines, topped by new age guitar supersonics, which became even more prominent after Vivian Campbell added his licks to the track when it was eventually issued as the last single from the album in America. "Definitely the last, we don't want to ram Whitesnake down people's throats," said Coverdale.

The new LP's standout track was the dynamic 'Still Of The Night', although Neil Murray listened in vain for some of the bass and guitar lines he and Sykes had laid down. "There are lots of bits Sykes recorded that never made it, or were moved, there's a bit where the solo is moved from one part to another. The original idea was to be even more Zeppelin-ish and have a sort of middle section from 'Whole Lotta Love' with all sorts of weird guitar stuff, then it ended up being a vocal part.'' In fact the middle vocals had been taped on the sly by Olsen when Coverdale was just limbering up.

The Zeppelin comparisons were certainly hard to ignore but didn't detract from the performance. After all, even the mighty Zeppelin could hardly claim total originality on their early material. By May the album was in the American Top Five where it would remain for nearly a year. It is hard to ignore the statistics, for even in an age when multi-platinum albums are becoming more and more frequent, Whitesnake still turned a few heads with sales of this record.

Away from the congratulations Neil Murray and Aynsley Dunbar, although credited on the album cover, had to engage lawyers to ensure their share of the royalties. In America the reworked single 'Here I Go Again' shot to the top of the charts after being leapt upon by radio stations, while back in Britain the lengthier and seemingly less commercial 'Still Of The Night' did well as a first single. Once it was clear that the album was going to be big, Coverdale was at last able to offer those concerned a chance to work as a live band.

Left: Sarzo and Vandenberg provide a new focal point, 1987 tour.
Right: Is This Love? Coverdale and fiancée Tawny Kittaen.

The line-up that emerged (perhaps not surprisingly) was the one that had shot the video, while Tawny Kittaen who provided much of the distracting footage in the clips became engaged to David Coverdale. Star of the sleeve for Ratt's 'Out Of The Cellar' album as well as some dubious B-movies, she met Coverdale at La Dome, a restaurant in LA. He saw her some time later on a US soap called Capitol and called her up. Coincidentally they were about to cast the band's videos and director Marty Callner saw she was right for the job. "Then it became a case of life imitating art, they fell in love on the set, I could see it happening."

At first Rudy Sarzo was unsure about leaving Quiet Riot whom he had rejoined. He left temporarily to work with Whitesnake and agreed to do the US support tour but Coverdale managed to persuade him to stay on. "I told David that I had every intention of returning to Quiet Riot as soon as my commitment to Whitesnake was completed. After all Quiet Riot and I go all the way back to 1978, there's a lot of attachment there for me, but then I realised that I had to look ahead not behind

The Whitesnake arm-pit salute again!

me. It wasn't fair to them if I couldn't give them all my energy and it wasn't fair to Whitesnake either. I had to make a decision and that was to stay part of Whitesnake. David has made it clear that he intends to keep this line-up together as long as possible. That's all I was waiting to hear.''

In fact Coverdale had already sent their management warning telegrams. ''I said if he breaks the other leg then they can have him.'' It also seemed as if David Coverdale had realised his mistakes in financial areas, problems which had destabilised the last line-up of the band. ''There was a serious imbalance in wages. I took care of certain people too well and others not as well as I should have, which will never, ever happen again.''

While Whitesnake seemed assured of success on vinyl, problems which had dogged the group ever since their inception continued to arise. Rudy Sarzo managed to break his foot (hence the telegram threat) in a bike accident back home in LA just before the band were due to play their first concert, débuting before 80,000

people at the annual Texas Jam festival. Sarzo had to do the show with a plaster cast on.

Despite this Whitesnake hit the road, opening for Motley Crue in America in June/July with a 45-minute slot based around the last two albums. 'Slide It In', benefiting from the chart action of the new one actually reappeared in the US charts, while a low-key reissue of many of Whitesnake's earlier albums not long after also did healthy business. Going out as a support was arranged well before the album zoomed up the charts. By the time it began the supporting act were in danger of overshadowing their headliners, such was the phenomenal success of the record. During a record store sign-in in Minneapolis 1500 people turned up.

The pairing of Whitesnake and Crue seemed a little incongruous at first, especially to Europeans, but in another concession to the business, Coverdale had updated his image. The black T-shirts and jeans of three years ago were consigned to the bin; the rest of his new band were fashionably glam anyhow. Given the album's sales it would've been hard for the band to put a step wrong and their short but sharp opening slot merely whetted people's appetites for a full-scale set.

Towards the end of the Motley Crue tour, Coverdale began to suffer again, this time from a stomach illness, but the work kept on and was rewarded handsomely. ''We've got the pleasure of remaining longer in the Top Five than anybody, including Bon Jovi. We've sold six million albums world-wide and it's still going,'' he added incredulously.

Whitesnake's role as a support act finished in Montreal at the tail end of October. They were already bigger than the headliners although the two bands got on well together throughout the tour. During Crue's encore Coverdale came on to celebrate a highly successful series of dates by doing 'Jailhouse Rock' with them. Whitesnake then spent a few weeks getting a full length set together and set out as headliners in early December in America, although they had already done a few bill topping shows there. ''The Motleys took a break. Financially it was going to be a strain for us so we did two headline shows in Michigan and broke records. Very rewarding.'' The stomach virus persisted though and in the end the start of the European tour in Germany and Sweden was cancelled, leaving time for him to rest up for the long awaited British gigs in December.

The Return Of The Snakes Tour was sold out within days, the band adding an extra show at Wembley on New Year's Eve, taking it to three nights in a row to cope with the demand. Ironically, their support for the tour was MSG, now renamed the MacCauley Schenker Group, with whom Coverdale had contemplated an alliance a few years before.

The audiences ranged from old faithfuls through to a new generation of fans to whom 'Whitesnake '87' might just as well have been a début album. It's hardly surprising that they're reported to have won Best New Act in some polls and the T-shirts, ranging from Here Comes Trouble, through the Donington Whitesnake Commando's fatigues, up to the latest (and somewhat more costly) designs featuring the band's new logo, reflected their long career on this side of the pond. As the band flew in, it was almost 10 years to the day since Whitesnake held those first auditions in London.

As if to emphasise the new look, the set concentrated almost entirely on the new album and its predecessor 'Slide It In', (along with a cover version of ZZ Top's retitled 'Tits') with only the band's 10-year-old anthem 'Ain't No Love In The Heart Of The City' to remind people of the past. While older fans were disappointed, the set was basically designed around material that would be familiar to an American audience. With the older albums beginning to surface there, Coverdale promised to dig back a little further into the band's repertoire next time around.

Once the brief British tour was over, the band were back to America, MTV awards, register to vote TV commercials and a headlining tour with Great White. If Whitesnake had been guilty of neglecting America in the past, it wasn't going to happen again. Starting in late January, the band were set for three months on the road before thoughts were to turn once again to a new album. Would the touring band make it on to vinyl was the question everyone was asking at the start of the tour. "I would hope so but it takes two to tango. I wasn't even intending to use the stage band in the studio but everybody's playing so good. I would like to try to keep us together but not at any price."

By the time the band were half way through their headlining tour of 1988 with their fourth American hit single, the mood of cautious optimism had been replaced by a definite affirmative. One thing was for sure, it would be somewhat quicker in the making. "It won't take as long next time, my nerves couldn't stand it."

True to his word, the album was wrapped up over the next 12 months, but if Coverdale prayed for a somewhat easier ride this time round, his pleas went unanswered, and the road to the album's eventual completion, though quicker, was still far from straight and narrow.

The initial period of writing must have been a worrying time, given the pressure to emulate the success of 'Whitesnake '87'. Ensconced in a pre-production facility in Lake Tahoe, Nevada, not far from where he had set up home, Coverdale's thoughts drifted back to his old writing partner Bernie Marsden, with whom he had collaborated on some of the band's most commercial material. Indeed, Whitesnake's current status owed more than a little to 'Here I Go Again', which Marsden had created for the 'Saints An' Sinners' album.

Since his departure from Whitesnake, Bernie's own career had been ticking over with varying degrees of success. Spells with his own groups Alaska and SOS, followed by a short stint in MGM alongside two other former Whitesnake players, Mel Galley and Neil Murray, failed to make much impact. Bernie had also been busy writing and working in the studio with the likes of Duran Duran's Andy Taylor and Deep Purple vocalist Ian Gillan. He had also been doing his own demos, with thoughts of a possible third solo album in the future. During early 1988, a batch of his demos sounded not unlike his old Whitesnake compositions. "They all had that old Whitesnake feel, so I decided to contact David via a letter," he told *RAW* magazine. Eventually the demos did indeed reach Coverdale, and the timing couldn't have been better.

While Coverdale was making overtures to one

America, 1987.

former Whitesnake guitarist, the P45's were on their way to another, and the first casualty of the 1987 touring line-up turned out to be Vivian Campbell. 'Musical differences' ran the press release, and maybe for once they at least got it partly right, for Campbell's style hadn't always meshed with the American sound Whitesnake had been striving for. In any case he was far from distraught, and quickly teamed up with an LA group called River Dogs, with whom he had already been working in a production capacity during his Whitesnake days.

Further news on the personnel front came with the announcement that Don Airey was being promoted to the ranks of a full-time Whitesnake member, following his important contributions to the foundations of the 1987 album. With these minor changes, the band retired to the Little Mountain studios once more to begin the new album during 1988 with producer Bruce Fairburn. The idea was to employ his services for the basic tracks, with the possibility of using others for the final production work. Twelve tracks were written, in

Whitesnake quickly out-shone their headliners as 1987 album went Platinum across America.

addition to which Geffen put forward another batch of golden Whitesnake oldies which they felt deserved the revamping treatment – 'We Wish You Well', the band's traditional set closer during the seventies, 'Don't Break My Heart Again' and 'Fool For Your Loving'. The last two were among the best numbers the old band had laid down, and their most successful. Whitesnake also agreed to do a take of 'Burning Heart', a Vandenburg original which David had long admired.

Replacing Campbell wasn't an urgent task. Feelers were put out to Jake E. Lee, Ozzie Osbourne's guitarist, but Lee was more interested in his new band Badlands. The problem became more acute with the temporary grounding of Vandenburg with an injured tendon, which developed problems and required surgery. As he and Coverdale had been the main writing team for the material, it was obviously a big disappointment for Vandenburg to be unable to continue with the album.

As the recording moved into the second phase, with Keith Olsen now handling the project, Coverdale managed to pull off quite a coup in rock terms by

securing the services of David Lee Roth's guitarist Steve Vai, widely regarded as one of the top players in the current generation of American guitarists. He began work almost at once on the album in his own LA studio. To ensure the minimum of delay, Whitesnake had in fact employed the services of a young guitarist called Kevin Russell to lay down a series of guitar guide tracks. This technique, often used during the sixties to provide help for tone deaf vocalists who looked the part but couldn't sing, enabled Vai to lay down his solos as soon as the ink on the contract had dried in March.

All these upsets did little to slow the album's progress. The lessons of 1987 had been well and truly learned, and obstacles were simply either overcome or bypassed when, in the past, they had put a complete halt on proceedings. With the album still more or less on schedule for a projected late July release, there was still one more twist in the Whitesnake tale.

Back in Britain, Glenn Hughes, Deep Purple's bassist during the years when Coverdale had been their vocalist, was taking time out at his parents'

house, avoiding the pressures which surrounded him in America where he had been living. After seeing Deep Purple out with Coverdale, the pair had gone their separate ways. Coverdale had set out on the long road to take Whitesnake to the top, Hughes had set up home in America and largely frittered his time (and money) away. It was only towards the end of the eighties that he finally began to conquer a drug problem and started to rebuild his career. This included an excellent album in partnership with Pat Thrall, work with Europe's old guitarist John Norum, a somewhat uncomfortable spell doing vocals for Black Sabbath, and a fruitful stint working alongside Gary Moore. Sadly that had broken down, and by 1989 Hughes was considering his options. Whatever they were, they certainly didn't count the idea of working again with David Coverdale among them. Yet he arrived home one day to learn that Geffen wanted to talk to him about doing just that.

Geffen were impressed with Glenn's vocal demos for another of their signings, ex-Whitesnake guitarist John Sykes' Blue Thunder. Indeed only shortage of time

and fears of running over budget prevented Hughes doing the vocals on the finished album.

The outcome of the transatlantic phone-calls was a contract for Glenn Hughes to contribute backing vocals to the (by now largely completed) Whitesnake album, aiming to build into it something of the unique vocal harmony sound which had made such a marked impression on Deep Purple back in 1974 with the 'Burn' album. While the tie-up was envisaged strictly as a studio one, Hughes was more than happy to take part, seeing it as final proof that his rehabilitation was complete. Pausing only to celebrate by doing a secret show in his home town of Cannock, in which he teamed up with his old sparring partner Mel Galley for a blistering set of Trapeze oldies, Glenn Hughes was off to make his own contributions to the Whitesnake story.

It's a story which probably has many more chapters to run, but which, thanks to the clout given him by the incredible success of the 1987 album, Coverdale is now finally able to guide more surely than at any time in his long and eventful musical career.

FAMILY TREE

February 1978 – March 1978
David COVERDALE vocals, **Bernie MARSDEN** guitar,
Micky MOODY guitar, **Neil MURRAY** bass,
Brian JOHNSTON keyboards, **David DOWLE** drums.

April 1978 – July 1978
David COVERDALE vocals, **Bernie MARSDEN** guitar,
Micky MOODY guitar, **Neil MURRAY** bass,
Pete SOLLEY keyboards, **David DOWLE** drums.

August 1978 – July 1979
David COVERDALE vocals, **Bernie MARSDEN** guitar,
Micky MOODY guitar, **Neil MURRAY** bass,
Jon LORD keyboards **David DOWLE** drums.

July 1979 – December 1981
David COVERDALE vocals, **Bernie MARSDEN** guitar,
Micky MOODY guitar, **Neil MURRAY** bass,
Jon LORD keyboards, **Ian PAICE** drums.

| WHITESNAKE Mk 1. |
| WHITESNAKE Mk 2. |
| WHITESNAKE Mk 3. |
| WHITESNAKE Mk 4. |
| WHITESNAKE Mk 5. |
| WHITESNAKE Mk 6. |
| WHITESNAKE Mk 7. |
| WHITESNAKE Mk 8. |
| WHITESNAKE Mk 9. |

October 1982 – December 1983
David COVERDALE vocals, **Mel GALLEY** guitar,
Micky MOODY guitar, **Colin HODGKINSON** bass,
Jon LORD keyboards, **Cozy POWELL** drums.

December 1983 – April 1984
David COVERDALE vocals, **Mel GALLEY** guitar,
John SYKES guitar, **Neil MURRAY** bass, **Jon LORD**
keyboards, **Cozy POWELL** drums.

June 1984 – January 1985
David COVERDALE vocals, **John SYKES** guitar,
Neil MURRAY bass, **Cozy POWELL** drums,
Richard BAILEY keyboards off-stage.

August 1985 – March 1986
David COVERDALE vocals, **John SYKES** guitar,
Neil MURRAY bass, **Aynsley DUNBAR** drums Line-up
existed only to record

February 1987 –
David COVERDALE vocals, **Vivian CAMPBELL**
guitar, **Adrian VANDENBERG** guitar, **Rudy SARZO**
bass, **Tommy ALDRIDGE** drums.

DAVID COVERDALE / WHITESNAKE
DISCOGRAPHY

The following material was recorded officially for use by radio stations only. Only limited numbers were pressed and they were unavailable to the general public although copies can sometimes be found at second hand stores or record fairs.

WHITESNAKE – IN CONCERT
Side one: Walking In The Shadow Of The Blues/ Ain't No Love In The Heart Of The City/ Steal Away/Belgian Tom's Hat Trick
Side two: Mistreated/ Lovehunter/ Breakdown
Reading Festival August 26, 1979.
GREAT BRITAIN: BBC Transcription CN 03440/S: November 1979

WHITESNAKE – IN CONCERT
Side one: Sweet Talker/ Walking In The Shadow/ Ain't Gonna Cry No More/ Lovehunter
Side two: Mistreated inc Soldier Of Fortune/ Ain't No Love In The Heart Of The City/ Fool For Your Loving
Reading Festival August 24, 1980.
GREAT BRITAIN: BBC Transcription CN 03682/S: November 1980
AMERICA: London Wavelength 201: 1980

THE BEST OF THE BBC ROCK HOUR
Side one: Sweet Talker/Lovehunter/Ain't No Love In The Heart Of The City
Side two: Highway Star/Strange Kind Of Woman/ Smoke On The Water
Reading Festival August 24, 1980.
AMERICA: London Wavelength 525: Air July 17, 1984

One side of Whitesnake and the other side of Deep Purple from a 1972 BBC In Concert.

WHITESNAKE AND LITA FORD – IN CONCERT
Side one: Gambler/ Guilty Of Love/ Love Ain't No Stranger/Walking In The Shadow Of The Blues/ Ready An' Willing.
Side two: Lita Ford set.
Spokane Washington October 12, 1984.
AMERICA: Westwood One IC 84.22: 1984

VARIOUS

READING ROCK VOLUME 1
Mean Records MNLP 82: UK: 1982
Contained one Whitesnake track, 'Walking In The Shadow Of The Blues', recorded at Reading, August 1979 and unavailable elsewhere officially. The rest of the album contained tracks by other groups taped at the 1982 festival.

DAVID COVERDALE AND WHITESNAKE
BAK 2049: UK: 1987
Interview picture disc, not officially sanctioned, but legal.

The Best of BBC Rock Hour

Reading Rock, Volume 1

The Wizard's Convention

Ready 'n Willing '80

WHITESNAKE – THE CHRIS TETLEY INTERVIEWS
CT 1006: UK: 1987.
Interview picture disc.

COMPANY
We Wish You Well/Right Time For Love
United Artists BP 326: UK: November 1979
Two Whitesnake tracks recorded by a session band
including some members of Whitesnake (see text).

YOUNG AND MOODY
All The Good Friends/Playing Your Game
Fabulous Records JC 3: UK: 1980
B-side written by Young/Moody/Coverdale and
produced by Roger Glover.

BERNIE MARSDEN – AND ABOUT TIME TOO
Parlophone PCS 7215: UK 1980
Original Japanese issue had a writing credit for Bobby
Dazzler – alias David Coverdale. This had gone by the
time it appeared in Britain.

BARBIE BENTON – AIN'T IT JUST THE WAY
Playboy PB 420: UK 1978
One song on this one-time Playboy pin-ups album
co-written by Coverdale.

THE WIZARD'S CONVENTION
RCA Victor RS 1085: UK: 1976
Vocals on one song 'Money To Burn' by Coverdale.
Also featured Roger Glover, Jon Lord, Glenn Hughes
and others.

BOOTLEGS

A CELEBRATION OF APATHY
Single album from Japan, recorded from crowd at
Reading Festival, August 26, 1979.

READY 'N' WILLING 80
Double album again from Japan, taped from the
audience in Tokyo, Japan, April 1980.

LIVE WITH THE CHOIR
Double album, this audience recording is probably from
the 1981 UK tour.

THE DEEP PURPLE OLD BOYS CLUB
A triple album set, issued in Japan. Audience recording
from Japan, June 1981 tour in colour sleeve.

SAINTS AN' SINNERS TOUR 82-83
Another Japanese triple set, probably recorded there in
February 1983, though the sleeve says Newcastle City
Hall, December 14, 1982.

HAMMERSMITH ODEON PART ONE
Single album recorded Hammersmith Odeon,
January 6, 1983, pressed in Europe.

HAMMERSMITH ODEON PART TWO
Single album recorded Hammersmith Odeon,
January 6, 1983, companion to above.

LIVE PALAIS DE BEAULIEU, LOSANNA
Single album recorded at Losanna, Switzerland, January 22, 1983, colour sleeve.

WINE, WOMEN AND WHITESNAKE
Single album from Europe, taken from the TV show in Ludwigshafen, Germany, March 19, 1983. Free poster in early copies.

DAVID SHOUTS
Single LP from same TV show but very poor quality.

HAMMERSMITH ODEON
Single album recorded in the crowd at the Hammersmith Odeon, April 1, 1983.

LIVE IN JAPAN
Double album, from Japan, probably taped there February, 1983.

WHITESNAKE – MONSTERS OF ROCK
Double album pressed in Sweden, recorded in Stockholm, April 14, 1984.

GUILTY OF LOVE
Single album recorded during band's 1984 American support tour.

STILL OF THE NIGHT
Single album recorded in Battlecreek, Michigan, July 26, 1987, colour sleeve.

ACTION
Double set recorded at Wembley, March 3, 1984 and Providence, August 8, 1987.

Bootlegs are illegal albums taken from tape recordings or TV performances, people are warned that many contain poorly pressed, edited or recorded material.

The Deep Purple Appreciation Society publishes two discographies which may be of interest to vinyl junkies. The first covers Deep Purple themselves including David Coverdale's work with the group. The second covers the splinter groups and the discography here was adapted from that. For details of these, please write to the author at the address at the beginning of the book.

British and American 7-inch and 12-inch singles, EP's and CD's
(PS) – picture sleeve with photograph/s on.
(AS) – art sleeve with graphics on.
If neither, then disc had a plain or generic record company sleeve only.

SINGLES

HOLE IN THE SKY/ BLINDMAN
Purple PUR 133: UK: May 1977.

BREAKDOWN/ ONLY MY SOUL
Purple PUR 136: UK: February 1978.

AIN'T NO LOVE IN THE HEART OF THE CITY
(stereo)/(mono)
Mirage WTG 3794: USA: 1978 promo.

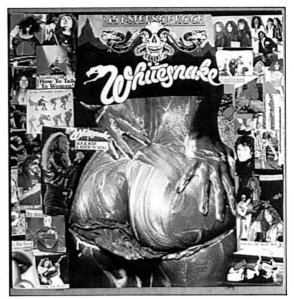
Monsters of Rock

Breakdown

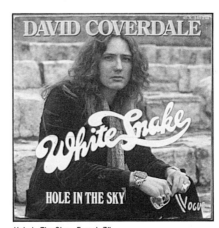
Hole In The Sky – French 7"

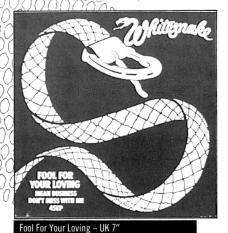

Fool For Your Loving – UK 7"

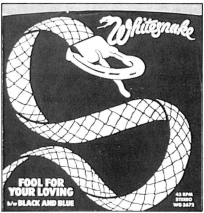

Fool For Your Loving – US 7"

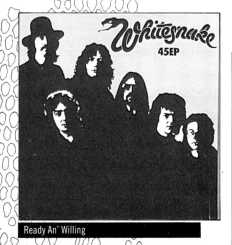

Ready An' Willing

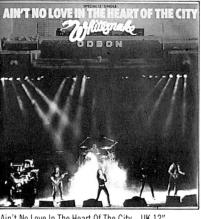

Ain't No Love In The Heart Of The City – UK 12"

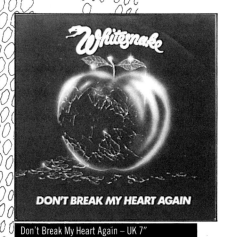

Don't Break My Heart Again – UK 7"

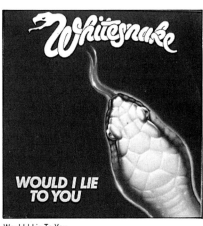

Would I Lie To You

**AIN'T NO LOVE IN THE HEART OF THE CITY
(stereo)/(mono)**
United Artists UA-X 1240Y: USA: 1978 promo
(studio version from 'Snakebite').

**AIN'T NO LOVE IN THE HEART OF THE CITY/
BLOODY MARY**
United Artists UA-X 1240Y: USA: 1978.

LIE DOWN/ DON'T MESS WITH ME
EMI International INT 568: UK: 1978.

THE TIME IS RIGHT FOR LOVE (stereo)/(mono)
United Artists UA-X 1291: USA: 1978 promo.

**THE TIME IS RIGHT FOR LOVE/ BELGIAN TOM'S
HAT TRICK**
United Artists UA-X 1291: USA: 1978.

THE TIME IS RIGHT FOR LOVE/ COME ON (live)
EMI International INT 578: UK: March 1979.

**LONG WAY FROM HOME/ TROUBLE/ AIN'T NO
LOVE IN THE HEART OF THE CITY (both live)**
United Artists BP 324: UK: October 1979 (AS)
33 1/3 rpm.

LONG WAY FROM HOME/ TROUBLE (live)
United Artists BP 324 DJ: UK: October 1979 promo
45 rpm.
All above live tracks later appeared on 'Live In The
Heart Of The City'.

LONG WAY FROM HOME (stereo)
United Artists UA X 1323Y: USA: 1979 promo.

LONG WAY FROM HOME/ WE WISH YOU WELL
United Artists UA X 1323Y: USA: 1979.

SWEET TALKER (stereo)/(mono)
Mirage WTG 3766: USA: 1980 promo.

SWEET TALKER/ AIN'T GONNA CRY NO MORE
Mirage WTG 3766: USA: 1980.

**FOOL FOR YOUR LOVING/ MEAN BUSINESS/
DON'T MESS WITH ME**
United Artists BP 352: UK: April 1980. (As limited
edition luminous, then non luminous).

FOOL FOR YOUR LOVING (long 4.04)/(short 3.30)
Mirage WG 3672: USA: 1980 promo.

FOOL FOR YOUR LOVING/ BLACK AND BLUE
Mirage WG 3672: USA: 1980 (AS).

**READY AN' WILLING/ NIGHTHAWK (Vampire
Blues)/ WE WISH YOU WELL**
United Artists BP 363: UK: July 1980 (AS).

**AIN'T NO LOVE IN THE HEART OF THE CITY
(live)/ TAKE ME WITH YOU (live)**
Sunburst/Liberty BP 381: UK: November 1980 12-inch
and edited 7-inch (PS).
From Hammersmith 1980, A-Side on US edition of LP,
B-Side on US and UK LP.

DON'T BREAK MY HEART AGAIN/ CHILD OF BABYLON
Liberty BP 399: UK: April 1981 (AS)
Liberty TC BP 395: UK: 1985 cassingle.

DON'T BREAK MY HEART AGAIN/ LONELY DAYS LONELY NIGHTS
Mirage WTG 3844: USA: 1981.

WOULD I LIE TO YOU/ GIRL
Liberty BP 399: UK: June 1981 (AS).

HERE I GO AGAIN/ BLOODY LUXURY
Liberty BP 416: UK: November 1982 (AS)
Liberty BBP 416: UK: November 1982 limited edition picture disc.
Liberty UA 895: USA: 1982.

GUILTY OF LOVE/ GAMBLER
Liberty BP 420: UK: August 1983 7-inch (PS)
Liberty BPP 420: UK: August 1983 limited edition Coverdale shaped picture disc.
Both later re-recorded for LP, these versions unavailable elsewhere.

LOVE AN' AFFECTION/ VICTIM OF LOVE
Liberty BP 418: UK: scheduled for December 13, 1984 but cancelled, acetates exist.

GIVE ME MORE TIME/ NEED YOUR LOVE SO BAD
Liberty BP 422: UK: January 1984 (PS) 7-inch or 12-inch.
'Need Your Love' was an album out-take featuring just Coverdale and Lord.

STANDING IN THE SHADOW/ ALL OR NOTHING (US album mix)
Liberty BP 423: UK: April 1984 7-inch (PS). Liberty BPP 423: UK: April 1984 Ltd Ed 7,000 copies picture disc.

SLOW AN' EASY (long)/(short)
Geffen PRO-A-2155: USA: 1984 (AS) promo only 12-inch.

LOVE AIN'T NO STRANGER (long)/(short)
Geffen PRO-A-2178: USA: 1984 (AS) promo only 12-inch.

LOVE AIN'T NO STRANGER (mono)/(stereo)
Geffen 7.29171: USA: 1984 promo only 7-inch.

LOVE AIN'T NO STRANGER/ GUILTY OF LOVE
Geffen 7.29171: USA: 1984 7-inch (PS)
Naturally all US issues off 'Slide It In' feature US LP mixes.

LOVE AIN'T NO STRANGER (US album mix)/ SLOW AN' EASY (US album mix).
Liberty BP 424: UK: January 1985 7-inch (PS).
First batch had free patch inside.
Liberty BP12 424: UK: 12-inch (PS). Very limited edition.

Here I Go Again – UK 7"

Here I Go Again – UK 7" Picture Disc

Give Me More Time

Slow An' Easy

Guilty Of Love – UK 7" Picture Disc

Love Ain't No Stranger – US 12" Promo

Love Ain't No Stranger – UK 12"

Still Of The Night – US 12" Promo

Still Of The Night – UK 7" White Vinyl

The vast range of special editions issued by UK record companies, many in very small quantities, reached epidemic proportions at this time. We think we've got them all listed.

STILL OF THE NIGHT (ext)/HERE I GO AGAIN '87/ YOU'RE GONNA BREAK MY HEART AGAIN
12EMI 5606: UK: March 1987 (AS) 12-inch.
12EMIS 5606: UK: March 1987 (AS) 12-inch with sheet of silver stickers inside.
12EMIP 5606: UK: March 1987 limited edition 12-inch picture disc.

STILL OF THE NIGHT/ HERE I GO AGAIN '87
EMI 5605: UK: March 1987 (AS Card or paper) 7-inch.
EMIW 5606: UK: March 1987 (AS) 7-inch Ltd Ed white vinyl with free poster.

STILL OF THE NIGHT/ STILL OF THE NIGHT
Geffen PRO-A-2650: USA: 1987 (AS) 12-inch only promo.
Geffen 28331: USA: 1987 7-inch promo (same 3.58 edit both sides).

STILL OF THE NIGHT/ DON'T TURN AWAY
Geffen 20694: USA: 1987 12-inch (with logo and titles on sticker) or 7-inch no sleeve. Cassette single too.

STILL OF THE NIGHT/ HERE I GO AGAIN '87
Geffen: USA: 1987 Promotional compact disc.

IS THIS LOVE/ STANDING IN THE SHADOWS '87/ NEED YOUR LOVE SO BAD '87.
EMI 12EM 3: UK: May 18, 1987 (PS) 12-inch black vinyl.
EMI 12EMW 3: UK: May 18, 1987 (PS) 12-inch white vinyl.

IS THIS LOVE/ STANDING IN THE SHADOWS '87/ NEED YOUR LOVE SO BAD '87.
EMI 12EMP 3: UK: May 18, 1987. Limited edition picture disc with stand shaped disc. 'Need Your Love' listed on disc but missed off by mistake, so it was issued on a one sided 7-inch inside (PSR 499) plus note explaining why the B-side '87 versions use original vocals with newly recorded backings/mixes by Keith Olsen.

IS THIS LOVE/STANDING IN THE SHADOWS '87
EMI EMX 3: UK: May 18, 1987 (poster sleeve) 7-inch.
EMI EM 3: UK: May 18, 1987 (PS) 7-inch.

IS THIS LOVE/ STANDING IN THE SHADOWS '87/ NEED YOUR LOVE SO BAD '87/ STILL OF THE NIGHT
EMI CDEM3: UK: 1987 compact disc.

IS THIS LOVE LP/ IS THIS LOVE (edit)
Geffen PRO-A-2810: USA: 1987 (PS) 12-inch promo.

IS THIS LOVE/ BAD BOYS/ STANDING IN THE SHADOWS/ NEED YOUR LOVE SO BAD '87
Geffen 20754-3: USA: 1987 12-inch.
GEFFEN 9 20754.4: USA: 1987 cassette in long box.

Is This Love – UK Picture Disc

Is This Love – UK 12" White Vinyl

Is This Love – UK CD Single

Is This Love – US 12" Promo

Is This Love – US Cassette Single

HERE I GO AGAIN '87/ YOU'RE GONNA BREAK/ CHILDREN OF THE NIGHT
Geffen 9 20695.0: USA: 1987 12-inch (AS) free logo sticker.
Geffen 9 20695.1: USA: 1987 cassette single in long box.

HERE I GO AGAIN '87/ CHILDREN OF THE NIGHT
Geffen 7 28339: USA: 1987 7-inch (AS).

HERE I GO AGAIN '87 US/ engraved signature
EMP 35: UK: October 1987 7-inch (poster sleeve).

HERE I GO AGAIN '87 US/ GUILTY OF LOVE
10EMI 35: UK: November 1987 (10-inch white vinyl plus pic label).
EMI 35: UK: November 1987 7-inch (PS).

HERE I GO AGAIN '87/ GUILTY OF LOVE/ HERE I GO AGAIN (LP mix)
12EMI 35: UK: November 1987 12-inch (PS) UK tour dates on back.

GIVE ME ALL YOUR LOVE/ FOOL FOR YOUR LOVING/ DON'T BREAK MY HEART AGAIN/ HERE I GO AGAIN '87
EMI CDEM 23: UK: 1987 COMPACT DISC with snakeskin pattern.

HERE I GO AGAIN/ IS THIS LOVE
Geffen 7.21929: USA: 1988 7-inch 'Back To Back Hits' series.

GIVE ME ALL YOUR LOVE/ FOOL FOR YOUR LOVING/ DON'T BREAK MY HEART AGAIN
EMI 12EMW 23: UK: January 25, 1988 (PS) 12-inch white vinyl, large colour label. EMI 12EM 23: UK: January 25, 1988 (PS) 12-inch black vinyl. EMI 12EMP 23: UK: January 25, 1988 (Poster Sleeve) 12-inch picture disc.
EMI EMW 23: UK: January 25, 1988 7-inch white vinyl with card backing sheet.
EMI EM 23: UK: January 25, 1988 (PS) 7-inch black vinyl PS.

GIVE ME ALL YOUR LOVE (remix)/ STRAIGHT FROM THE HEART
Geffen 28103: USA: 1988 12-inch.
Vivian Campbell guitar added. 7-inch, 12-inch or cassingle.

ALBUMS

WHITESNAKE
Side one: Lady/ Blindman/ Goldie's Place/ Whitesnake
Side two: Time On My Side/ Peace Lovin' Man/ Sunny Days/Hole In The Sky/ Celebration
Recorded (backings) Kingsway August 1976, (vocals) Musicland September 1976.
UK: Purple TPS 3509: May 1977. Deleted.
Issued in single sleeve. Special record bag with lyrics, pics etc. Also released in Europe and Japan. Not issued in America.

Here I Go Again – US 12"

Here I Go Again – UK 10" White Vinyl

Here I Go Again – US Cassette Single

Give Me All Your Love – UK 7" White Vinyl

Give Me All Your Love – CD Maxi Single

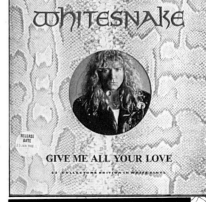

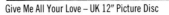
Give Me All Your Love – UK 12" Picture Disc

Give Me All Your Love – UK 12" White Vinyl

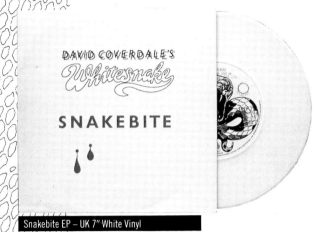
Snakebite EP – UK 7" White Vinyl

Snakebite Album – US Original

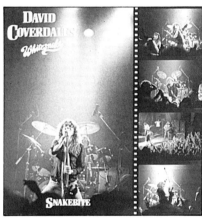
Snakebite Album – Dutch Edition

Trouble -- UK Original

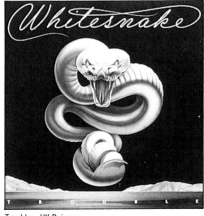
Trouble – UK Reissue

SNAKEBITE EP

Side one: Bloody Mary/ Steal Away
Side two: Ain't No Love In The Heart Of The City,
Come On
Recorded Central Studios London, April 1977.
UK: EMI International INEP 751: June 1978 (deleted).
Limited edition 7-inch – 15,000 in white (dog's milk)
vinyl with art sleeve, thereafter in black vinyl without
sleeve.

SNAKEBITE

Side one: Come On/ Bloody Mary/ Ain't No Love In
The Heart Of The City/ Steal Away
Side two: Keep On Giving Me Love/ Queen Of Hearts/
Only My Soul/ Breakdown
USA: United Artists LA 915: 1978 (deleted)
Issued in single sleeve. Special record bag with lyrics,
pics etc.
USA: Geffen XGHS 2417: 1987 (also on CD)
Reissue similar to original but with new cover
typography and logo.
HOLLAND: Sunburst 5C 062 61290: October 1978
deleted.
Single cover with live colour photos front and back,
plus special record bag.

TROUBLE

Side one: Take Me With You/ Love To Keep You
Warm/ Lie Down/Day Tripper/ Nighthawk
Side two: The Time Is Right For Love/ Trouble/ Belgian
Tom's Hat Trick/ Free Flight/ Don't Mess With Me
Recorded Central Recorders, London, May/June,
keyboards overdubbed August 1978.
UK: EMI International INS 3022: Oct 1978 deleted.
Issued in single textured sleeve, white with titles and
logo. Special record bag.
USA: Sunburst EMI UA LA 937: 1978 deleted.
Issued in single sleeve, airbrushed snake design.
UK: United Artists UAG 30305: September 1980
deleted.
Reissue with American cover design.
UK: Fame FA 3002 : May 1982.
Reissue with American cover art.
USA: Geffen 24175 : 1987 (also on CD). Reissue.

NORTHWINDS

Side one: Northwinds/ Keep On Giving Me Love/ Give
Me Kindness/ Time And Again
Side two: Queen Of Hearts/ Only My Soul/ Say You
Love Me/Breakdown
Recorded Air Studios, 1978.
UK: Purple TPS 3513 : March 10, 1978 deleted. Issued
in single sleeve. Special record bag with lyrics, pics etc.
First printing code on sleeve is G & L GL 7803, second
print code is EDT 7803, 1982 edition (with no inner
bag) code is G & L 8202.
UK: FAME FA 413097.1: April 1984. Reissue. No
inner bag.

LIVE IN HAMMERSMITH

Side one: Come On/ Might Just Take Your Life/ Lie
Down/Ain't No Love In The Heart Of The City
Side two: Trouble/ Mistreated
Recorded Hammersmith Odeon November 24, 1978.
JAPAN: Polydor Sunburst MPF 1288: March 1980.
Issued in single sleeve, lyric sheet inside.

Northwinds – Rejected Cover

LOVEHUNTER
Side one: Long Way From Home/ Walking In The
Shadow Of The Blues/ Help Me Thro' The Day/
Medicine Man/ You And Me
Side two: Mean Business/ Lovehunter/ Outlaw/ Rock
'n' Roll Women/ We Wish You Well
Recorded Clearwell Castle, Glos. and Central
Recorders, London, May-July 1979.
UK: United Artists UA 30264: October 1979 deleted.
Issued in single sleeve. Special record bag with lyrics,
pics etc.
UK: Fame FA 4130994: April 1984. Reissue, no bag.
USA: United Artists LT 981: 1979 deleted.
Single sleeve, sticker on front.
USA: Geffen : 1987 (also on CD). Reissue.

READY AN' WILLING
Side one: Fool For Your Loving/ Sweet Talker/ Ready
An' Willing/ Carry Your Load/ Blindman
Side two: Ain't Gonna Cry No More/ Love Man/ Black
And Blue/ She's A Woman
Recorded Ridge Farm and Central Recorders,
December 1979/February 1980.
UK: United Artists UAG 30302: June 1980 deleted.
Issued in single sleeve, silver background.
Special record bag.
UK: Fame FA 4313 41: September 1985. Reissue,
no inner bag.
USA: Mirage WTG 19276: 1980 deleted.
Single sleeve as UK with inner bag.

Northwinds

Live At Hammersmith

LIVE . . . IN THE HEART OF THE CITY
Side one: Come On/ Sweet Talker/ Walking In The
Shadow/Lovehunter
Side two: Fool For Your Loving/ Ain't Gonna Cry
No More/Ready An' Willing/ Take Me With You
Side three: Come On/ Might Just Take Your Life/ Lie
Down/Ain't No Love In The Heart Of The City
Side four: Trouble/ Mistreated
Sides one and two recorded Hammersmith Odeon
June 23/24, 1980.
Sides three and four Hammersmith Odeon
November 24, 1978.
UK: Sunburst SNAKE 1: November 1980 (CD 1987
omits four tracks). Issued in single sleeve. Credit/photo
sheet inside.
1978 LP same as Japanese issue above.
FRANCE: Carrere 67367: 1980.
Gatefold sleeve, art as UK.

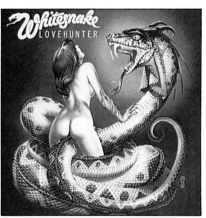

Lovehunter

Ready An' Willing

LIVE . . . IN THE HEART OF THE CITY
Side one: Come On/ Sweet Talker/ Walking In The
Shadow/Lovehunter
Side two: Ain't No Love In The Heart Of The City/Fool
For Your Loving/ Take Me With You
Recorded Hammersmith Odeon June 23/24, 1980.
USA: Mirage WTG 19292: January 1981 deleted.
Single sleeve and album with 'Ain't No Love', 1980
version (issued on 12-inch in UK) replacing two other
tracks.
USA: Geffen 24168: 1987 (also on CD). Reissue.

COME AN' GET IT
Side one: Come An' Get It/ Hot Stuff/ Don't Break
My Heart Again/ Lonely Days, Lonely Nights/ Wine,
Women And Song

Live . . . In The Heart Of The City – Double Album

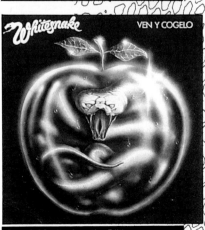

Come An' Get It – Argentine Edition

Come An' Get It – US Edition

Saints An' Sinners – UK Picture Disc

Slide It In - UK Picture Disc

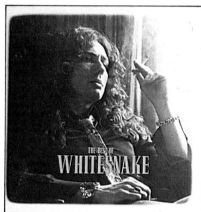
The Best Of Whitesnake – Dutch Edition

Slide It In – UK Edition

Side two: Child Of Babylon/ Would I Lie To You/ Girl/ Til The Day I Die
Recorded Startling Studios, Ascot July/September 1980/January 1981
UK: Liberty LBG 30327: April 1981
Issued in single sleeve. Special record bag with lyrics, pics etc.
USA: Mirage WTG 16043: 1981 deleted.
Single sleeve, snake's mouth airbrushed out.
No record bag.
USA: Geffen 24167: 1987 (also on CD). Reissue.

SAINTS AN' SINNERS
Side one: Young Blood/ Rough An' Ready/ Bloody Luxury/Victim Of Love/ Crying In The Rain
Side two: Here I Go Again/ Love An' Affection/ Rock An' Roll Angels/ Dancing Girls/ Saints An' Sinners
Recorded Rock City/ Shepperton/ Clearwell October 1981/January 1982. Vocals/mix Battery Studio September 1982.
USA: Liberty LBG 30354: November 1982.
Issued in single sleeve. Special record bag with lyrics, pics etc.
UK: Liberty LBG 30354: November 1982 deleted.
Limited Edition picture disc.

THE BEST OF WHITESNAKE
Side one: Walking In The Shadow Of The Blues/ Trouble/ Lie Down/ Sweet Talker/ Lovehunter
Side two: Don't Break My Heart Again/ Ain't No Love In The Heart Of The City/ Fool For Your Loving/ Take Me With You/We Wish You Well
JAPAN: Polydor 28MM 0088: 1982
(also on CD 1987).
Single sleeve, lyric sheet inside. Also issued in France, but not in UK.

THE GREATEST WHITESNAKE
Side one: Fool For Your Loving/ Walking In The Shadow Of The Blues/ Young Blood/ Lovehunter/ Trouble
Side two: Come An' Get It/ Sweet Talker/ Lie Down/ Til The Day I Die/ Take Me With You
Side three: Don't Break My Heart Again/ Ready An' Willing/Bloody Luxury/ Mean Business/ Wine Women And Song
Side four: Long Way From Home/ Ain't Gonna Cry No More/ Hot Stuff/ Here I Go Again/ We Wish You Well
JAPAN: Polydor 30MM 9244/5: 1983.
Gatefold sleeve. Issued only in Japan.

SLIDE IT IN
Side one: Gambler/ Slide It In/ Standing In The Shadow/Give Me More Time/ Love Ain't No Stranger
Side two: Slow An' Easy/ Spit It Out/ All Or Nothing/ Hungry For Love/ Guilty Of Love
Recorded Musicland Studios, Germany May/June and October/November 1983.
UK: Liberty LBG 2400001: January 1984
(also on CD 1988)
Issued in single sleeve, special record bag.
USA: Geffen GHS 4018: April 1984 (also on CD 1987).
Sleeve as UK. Tracks remixed, bass re-recorded and lead partially re-recorded, track order changed.
UK: Liberty LBG 24 0000 0: March 1985 deleted.
Picture disc limited edition, with US mixed tracks.

JAPAN: CBS Sony 32AP 2681: March 1984 deleted. Special limited edition, LP as UK, in a card bag, with 20 page booklet, a pendant, sticker, poster and lyric sheet.

SLIDE IT IN – SPECIAL VERSION
Side one: Slide It In/ Love Ain't No Stranger/ Guilty Of Love
Side two: Slow An Easy/ Gambler/ Need Your Love So Bad
JAPAN: Geffen 2AP 2966: 1985 deleted. Issued in single sleeve, art as normal but with gold picture frame around. Mini-album contains five US remixed tracks plus one non album B-side, plus interview with Coverdale talking about the songs, taped in Los Angeles Oct 3, 1984. Fold out sheet inside with tracks, lyrics and interview transcription.

Slide It In – Japanese Limited Edition

WHITESNAKE 1987 UK Edition
Side one: Still Of The Night/ Bad Boys/ Give Me All Your Love/ Looking For Love (Here I Go Again '87)
Side two: Crying In The Rain/ Is This Love/ Straight From The Heart/ Don't Turn Away/ Children Of The Night
Recorded Little Mountain September, October, December 1985, January, March 1986, London October 1986.
UK: EMI EMC 3528: April 1987 (deleted). Issued in single sleeve, Whitesnake logo embossed. Record bag has lyrics and logo. Not on US copy.
UK: EMI EMC 3528: 1987 deleted.
As above but not embossed.
UK: EMI CDP 746702: 1987 Compact Disc. Includes 'Here I Go Again '87' and 'You're Gonna Break My Heart Again' as extra tracks.
UK: EMI 3528: 1987 deleted.
Limited picture disc edition, nine tracks.
UK: EMI EMCX 3528 : 1987.
Reissue with 'Here I Go Again '87' added after it had been in UK charts.

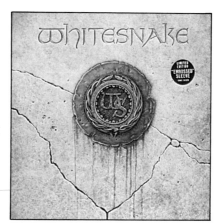

Slide It In - UK Picture Disc

WHITESNAKE 1987 US Edition
Side one: Crying In The Rain/ Bad Boys/ Still Of The Night/Here I Go Again
Side two: Give Me All Your Love/ Is This Love/ Children Of The Night/ Straight For The Heart/ Don't Turn Away
USA: Geffen XGHS 24099: April 1987 (also on 9-track CD)
Issued in single sleeve. Tracks rearranged to include one not originally on UK edition, though it was added later.

Best Whitesnake

BEST WHITESNAKE
Side one: Still Of The Night/ Don't Break My Heart Again/Only My Soul/ Blindman/ Guilty Of Love
Side two: Fool For Your Loving/ Lovehunter/ Here I Go Again/Ain't No Love In The Heart Of The City/ Day Tripper
GREECE: EMI Liberty 062 748 5481: 1987 (also on CD).

Whitesnake/Northwinds Reissue

WHITESNAKE/NORTHWINDS
UK: Connoisseur VSOP 118: May 1988 (also on CD)
Issued in gatefold, with art off both original sleeves. Same tracks.